FOUR PILLARS

Foreword by
DR. ALEX PHIRI

FOUR PILLARS

Essential Elements For Marriage

DOUGLAS ASANTE

ISBN: 978-1-916692-30-5

Published in the United Kingdom by
Equip Publishing House

To my beloved wife, Diana, whose love,
patience, and unwavering support remain
the heartbeat of my life and ministry.

This book is also dedicated to every couple longing to
build a godly home—May your marriage reflect Christ
and His Church. Above all, to the Lord Jesus Christ,
the true foundation of every lasting home.

CONTENTS

CHAPTER THREE

Unity **45**

Chapter Four

x

ENDORSEMENTS

Douglas Asante has given the Church a timeless treasure. *Four Pillars* is not just another book on marriage—it is a Spirit-filled guide that dismantles shaky foundations and rebuilds homes upon God's eternal blueprint. Every couple, whether preparing for marriage, newly-wed, or seasoned, will find in these pages the wisdom and strength to flourish.

REV. SAMUEL OPPONG-DRUYEH
Word Impact Faith International

"I found myself pausing, praying, and underlining entire sections. *Four Pillars* is deeply practical, yet profoundly theological. Douglas brings clarity to issues many couples struggle with but rarely confront. This book will not just inform you; it will transform the way you see your marriage."

PS SANDRA DELALI
Marriage and Family Therapist

Marriage is God's first institution, and this book restores honour to that truth. Douglas Asante writes with the authority of Scripture, the tenderness of a pastor, and the insight of one who has walked the journey. I wholeheartedly recommend this as a must-have for every Christian home.

PROPHETESS DOREEN KATTAH
The Lord's Heart Ministry

Four Pillars – The Essential Elements for Marriage by Pastor Douglas Asante is a profound and timely resource for anyone who values God's design for marriage. Drawing from years of pastoral experience, personal family life, and the discipline of a military career, Pastor Asante delivers practical and biblical truths with clarity and depth.

This book addresses the foundational pillars every marriage must stand on: Severance—understanding what it truly means to leave and cleave; Permanence—the sacredness of vows and lifelong commitment; Unity—building a love story rooted in oneness and spiritual harmony; and Intimacy—rediscovering true closeness in all its dimensions: spiritual, emotional, physical, and intellectual.

With real-life case studies, reflective questions, and practical applications, this book is not just theory but a hands-on guide. It is a must-have for married couples and those preparing for marriage. Your relationship will be enriched, strengthened, and transformed.

REV. HENRY GODSON-AFFUL
British Army Chaplain

"This is more than a book—it's a roadmap to covenant love. Severance, Permanence, Unity, and Intimacy are not just ideas in this book; they are living truths that, if embraced, will not only benefit your love but will revolutionise your marriage. I therefore recommend this book to every couple who wants to enjoy a lasting relationship."

ELDER CHARLES ANTO
Licensed Marriage Counsellor
Family Life Coach & Author

ACKNOWLEDGEMENTS

I give all glory and thanks to *the Lord*, whose grace and wisdom have sustained me through this journey. Without Him, these pages would be empty words.

To my dear wife, *Diana*—thank you for your love, encouragement, and prayers. You have been my greatest support and inspiration, and this work is as much yours as it is mine.

My heartfelt gratitude goes to *Dr. Alex Phiri* for graciously writing the foreword. Your wisdom and faith in this message have added depth and weight to this book.

I am also thankful for *my pastors, mentors, and friends* who have prayed with me, shared insights, and encouraged me along the way. Your voices and examples have strengthened my conviction that marriage is truly God's design for joy and purpose.

To *Equip Publishing House*, thank you for your partnership and care in bringing this work to life.

And finally, to *every reader*—thank you for opening your heart to these words. It is my prayer that this book will bless your marriage, refresh your faith, and remind you that with God at the centre, your home can truly become a place of love, unity, and joy.

FOREWORD

Marriage is one of the most beautiful and demanding callings God has entrusted to humanity. It is the very first institution He ordained, established even before the creation of the Church or the formation of nations. From the moment Adam looked upon Eve and declared her to be "bone of my bones and flesh of my flesh," marriage has been at the centre of God's design for human flourishing. It is meant to be a covenant of love, fidelity, and companionship, reflecting something of God's own covenantal nature. And yet, it is no secret that marriage is also one of the most fragile realities in our world today. Even among believers, many couples find themselves struggling with distance, conflict, and discouragement. The dream of marriage as a source of joy and blessing can easily be replaced with disappointment when its foundations are not properly understood or maintained.

It is into this space that Douglas Asante has offered a gift to the body of Christ. His book, *Four Pillars: Essential Elements For Marriage*, is not simply another voice among the many writing about relationships. It is a deeply biblical, carefully thought-through, and pastorally sensitive guide to what makes a marriage stand and what allows it to thrive. Douglas has chosen to frame his work around four pillars – Severance, Permanence, Unity, and Intimacy, and in doing so he has cut through the noise of countless quick-fix approaches. Instead of offering shallow advice or cultural trends dressed up in Christian language, he has returned to the blueprint that God Himself drew when He created marriage. These pillars are not optional enhancements; they are the very supports that hold up the covenant of husband and wife. Without them, the structure of marriage is unstable. With them, a couple can weather storms, grow together, and shine as a testimony of God's love.

The first pillar, Severance, is perhaps the least understood but one of the most essential. The Bible is unambiguous in Genesis when it says that a man shall leave his father and mother and be joined to his wife. This act of leaving is not an abandonment of parents or a denial of our duty to honour them. Rather, it is a reordering of priorities, a recognition that once marriage begins, the new family unit takes precedence. Many couples today continue to stumble here. Emotional dependence on parents, financial entanglement, or undue influence from in-laws can quietly erode the foundation of a marriage. Douglas addresses this with balance, showing how couples can and must establish independence while still walking in respect and love for their parents. It is a liberating truth, because it clears the ground for a marriage to flourish in its own right rather than forever being entangled in the expectations of others.

From there, Douglas turns to the second pillar, Permanence. In a culture where contracts can be dissolved with the click of a button and commitments are often made lightly, the biblical vision of permanence stands as a stark contrast. Marriage is not meant to be an arrangement of convenience but a covenant of lifelong fidelity. Jesus Himself declared, "What God has joined together, let no one separate." Douglas does not shy away from the reality that marriages face hardships, financial strain, health crises, betrayals of trust – but he insists that the strength of permanence is what enables couples to endure these hardships rather than be undone by them. This vision is not naive; it is profoundly hopeful. To know that your spouse is committed to you for life is to be given the security in which trust, intimacy, and forgiveness can grow. Permanence anchors a marriage in stability and points beyond itself to the faithfulness of God, who never abandons His covenant with His people.

The third pillar is Unity. If severance clears the ground and permanence sets the strength, unity gives marriage its beauty. Douglas is clear that unity is not uniformity. It does not mean a husband and wife must think the same thoughts or erase their differences. Rather, it is the weaving together of two distinct lives into one shared purpose. It is choosing daily to work together, to communicate honestly, to lay aside pride and selfish ambition in favour of humility, patience, and mutual submission. Unity reflects the profound mystery Paul speaks of in Ephesians, where marriage becomes a picture of the relationship between Christ and the Church. In practice, it means husbands and wives learning to think together even when they do not think alike, learning to cherish differences as complementary rather than competitive, and building a shared identity that honours God. Douglas illustrates this with stories and examples that make it clear how easily unity can be threatened, but also how wonderfully it can be cultivated when both partners are intentional.

Finally, Douglas leads us into the fourth pillar, Intimacy. Too often, intimacy is reduced to physical expression alone. While physical closeness is an important and God-given aspect of marriage, intimacy is far richer. Douglas describes intimacy in four dimensions: emotional, intellectual, spiritual, and physical. True intimacy is about vulnerability, trust, and deep knowing. It is about a husband and wife sharing their inner lives with one another, praying together, learning together, delighting in each other. Intimacy is what transforms marriage from mere coexistence into a relationship of joy, delight, and strength. Many couples, he observes, may live under the same roof yet feel worlds apart. This book offers not only an explanation of why intimacy fades but also practical encouragement for how it can be restored and deepened. It is a hopeful call for marriages not to settle for cold distance, but to pursue the richness God intended.

Taken together, these four pillars form a compelling framework. They are not fads that will pass with time. They are not the private theories of one man. They are the enduring truths God Himself embedded into the covenant of marriage from the very beginning. And what makes this book unique is the way Douglas combines theological depth with practical wisdom. Each chapter is filled with Scripture, making it clear that this is God's word on marriage, not merely human opinion. But alongside the biblical teaching are case studies, reflection questions, and encouragements that make the principles immediately applicable. Readers are not left to admire the truths from a distance; they are invited to wrestle with them, to discuss them, and to live them out in their own homes.

I believe this book will be of immense value to many. For those preparing for marriage, it offers a roadmap that will save years of unnecessary heartache. For newlyweds, it provides strong foundations upon which to build. For couples who have been married for decades, it offers fresh reminders and encouragements to strengthen what already exists. And for those in struggling marriages, it shines as a light of hope, calling them back to God's design and showing them that restoration is possible. Pastors, counsellors, and mentors will also find it a resource to place in the hands of those they guide.

On a personal note, though I do not work with Douglas in daily ministry, I have always admired his clarity and faithfulness whenever our paths have crossed. This book reflects the same qualities: a commitment to Scripture, an attentiveness to the struggles couples face, and a refusal to compromise on truth. It is written not to impress but to serve, and that is what makes it so trustworthy. I have read many books on marriage, but this one stands out for its balance of theological grounding, pastoral sensitivity, and practical application. It is the kind of book that does not just inform the mind but challenges the heart and equips the hands.

As you begin to read, I encourage you not to rush. Let the words sink in. Talk through the questions with your spouse. Pray over the areas where you feel convicted or encouraged. Ask the Holy Spirit to illuminate your own marriage, to show you where you need to leave and cleave, where you need to recommit to permanence, where you need to pursue deeper unity, and where you need to cultivate intimacy. These are not abstract ideas; they are the realities upon which your home will stand or fall.

Marriage will never be effortless, but it can be glorious when it is built on God's design. With these four pillars in place, a couple can face storms without collapsing, can grow in joy through every season, and can stand as a testimony to the watching world of God's covenant love. That is why I wholeheartedly commend this book to you. It is timely, it is biblical, and it has the potential to transform not only individual marriages but entire families and communities.

My prayer is that as you read, you will discover that these pillars are not just theological concepts but living truths. May they strengthen your own home. May they remind you that your marriage is not merely about your happiness but about God's glory. And may they help you and your spouse to reflect, in your own imperfect yet grace-filled way, the beauty of Christ and His Church.

DR. ALEX PHIRI
Lead Minister, River of Life Community Church, Sheffield
Principal, Emmaus School of Theology, Sheffield

INTRODUCTION

The institution called marriage was God's intention for humanity since the very beginning of creation. God founded marriage, and He alone can sustain marriage.

"This explains why a man leaves his father
and mother and is joined by his wife,
and the two are united into one."
GENESIS 2:24 NLT

A marriage that excludes God is building on shaky ground and may struggle to stand the test of time. The truth is, you can only build a sustainable home, when you build with the builder Himself.

Your marriage is only as beautiful in proportion to how much of God you have allowed into your home. Once this truth is established in your heart, you will find yourself closer to a blissful home.

But then, why do you think some Christian homes still have certain issues? What do you think could be the cause of divorce in most Christian homes? How do people who used to love each other intimately, suddenly become enemies?

Many factors contribute to this, but the most outstanding factor is when a believer stops where God just started with them.

For instance, the Bible says,

> *"The fear of the LORD is the beginning*
> *of wisdom, and the knowledge of*
> *the Holy One is understanding."*
> PROVERBS 9:10

You see, the fear of God is just the beginning. Loving God is not all that makes a blissful home. It should not be a surprise that just being 'born again' is not enough to step into, and sustain, a successful marriage.

There are certain *things you need to know, principles you need to understand, and elements of marriage you must have* before you say, 'Yes, I do.'

Do you know what it takes to have a successful marriage? You would probably get a wide range of responses if you asked several couples. Even though their marriages are very different from one another, there are some similarities you will find among all strong Christian couples.

In the pages ahead, I invite you to journey with me through the four essential elements that form the foundation of a thriving, God-honouring marriage: **Severance, Permanence, Unity, and Intimacy.** Though often overlooked or misunderstood in many homes today, these timeless principles remain vital to the health and happiness of any marital union.

As we explore each element in depth, you'll discover practical wisdom, biblical truth, and heartfelt encouragement to strengthen your relationship. This isn't just theory—it's the pathway to experiencing the joy, fulfilment, and deep connection that God intended for marriage.

Yes, *heaven on earth* is possible in your home. As you embrace these truths and delight in your spouse, you'll find that marriage can truly be one of life's greatest blessings.

YOUR MARRIAGE IS ONLY AS BEAUTIFUL IN PROPORTION TO HOW MUCH OF GOD YOU HAVE ALLOWED INTO YOUR HOME

1

SEVERANCE

1

SEVERANCE

The foundation of marriage begins with severance—a concept, rooted in the biblical command:

> *"For this reason, a man shall*
> *leave his father and his mother..."*
> GENESIS 2:24[1]

The keyword, 'leave,' in the above context has its Hebrew root word *'aw-zab,'* which means to abandon, to leave poor, and to refuse. The word also means loosen bands, as if releasing a creature from its bonds.

This does not mean a man has to abandon his parents and isolate himself from them. It must be a wilful act, a

---

1 Genesis 2:24 (NKJV), The Holy Bible

choice, where the man separates himself in order to be independent of his parents. While this separation might not feel comfortable most times, as the man will have to take responsibility for his well-being and life, it is essential and as God commands it. Hence, the reason, severance is an essential element of marriage.

Consider this: In the same household, a man cannot be both an independent spouse, and a child who is dependent on the parent, all at the same time. No! *Priorities must remain clear, and boundaries must be set between childhood and manhood.* Therefore, the scripture above in Genesis 2:24, speaks about the man respectfully leaving his parent, to become independent – severance.

HENCE, SEVERANCE IS AN ESSENTIAL ELEMENT OF MARRIAGE

God's View of the Man

After several thoughts about the man that must leave, according to Genesis 2:24, my question is: What is God's view about man in marriage? Does severance of a male child from his parent make him man enough to take up a wife?

You see, when God wanted to create man, He had a picture at heart. The Bible says:

> *Then God said, "Let Us make man in Our image, according to Our likeness; let them have dominion*

over the fish of the sea, over the birds of the air,
and over the cattle, over all the earth and over
every creeping thing that creeps on the earth."
GENESIS 1:26[2]

There are qualities a man must possess which enable him to be in tune with the command of severance God gave in Genesis 2:24. These qualities are what give the man abilities to relinquish and disengage from where he had spent his childhood, to become independent first, before he cleaves to his wife – this will be discussed later in subsequent chapters.

A man before God is a person who is mature enough to lead others, under God's leadership of him. Before you can be man enough to stand independently, you must have learned the way of God, submitting to and saying, 'Yes' anytime He calls. No man is more man than the one who, under God, presides over things committed to his hands by God (Genesis 1:28).

Severance or the end of childhood happens when society (largely made up of parents) determines that you have reached an age where you can take responsibility for yourself in front of the community. Severance does not mean reckless independence or gallivanting around. Rather, severance is still a dependent approach, but now the dependence will be fully on God. Being able to handle wisely all that God has committed to one's hands.

---

2 Genesis 1:26 (NKJV), The Holy Bible

At the point of severance, you as a man must have become mature (in age and character), to make informed decisions and better choices, and become responsible for the consequences of your actions

However, does leaving now make you a child who forgets his parents? Of course not. Every male child who wants to enter the institution of Marriage must learn how to leave respectfully.

A MAN BEFORE GOD IS A PERSON WHO IS MATURE ENOUGH TO LEAD OTHERS, UNDER GOD'S LEADERSHIP OF HIM

RESPECTFULLY LEAVING YOUR PARENTS

"So then, they are no longer two but one flesh. Therefore what God has joined together, let not man separate."
MATTHEW 19:6 [3]

The command God gave for a man to leave and cleave to his wife was later addressed by Jesus. Frankly, Jesus further instructed that nobody is permitted to come between the man and his wife (Matthew 19:6). No one! No mother, father, relative, or in-laws are meant to separate a couple that made a vow to leave their parents and cleave together as one flesh. The instruction to leave is a clear one. Couples must learn to cut the ties, and, learn to do so respectfully.

---

3 Mathew 19: 6 (NKJV), The Holy Bible

Similarly, parents must also learn to respect their children's new home, by not acting as an intruder. Many parents don't seem to cut this tie easily, and this intrusion into their children's homes has become the reason for crises in several homes.

After our marriage ceremony, my darling wife and I walked together down the aisle of the church, symbolically declaring to the world that we had left our parents as God instructed, to begin our home together as one flesh. This symbolic declaration was to show that we were no longer dependent on our parents for emotional and financial support of any sort. Rather, we turn to each other as one because ours is now the most important relationship in our lives.

In marriage, when the father gives the bride to the groom, the relationship between the father and daughter is also severed. However, we see the consequences that follow when a daughter still has ties with her father, or vice versa. For instance, David received Michal, but Saul, her father, took her back later.

The Bible says:

> *"But Saul had given Michal, his daughter,*
> *David's wife, to Palti, the son of Laish,*
> *who was from Gallim."*
> I SAMUEL 25:44 [4]

The intention must be never to return to parental authority again. This does not mean that the couple must no longer

---

4 1 Samuel 25: 44 (NKJV), The Holy Bible

be honoured by the parents. Every parent should learn to respect the 'leaving' of their children. As a husband, being financially dependent on your wife's family robs you of your leadership role as the head of the family.

As a wife, reaching out to your friends or family members for emotional succour rather than talking to your husband about any issues will rob you of the love, peace, and togetherness you ought to share with your husband. Continued emotional dependence on a parent can also be destructive. Never make the mistake of allowing a third party to enter in between your severance from your parents.

RATHER, WE TURN TO EACH OTHER AS ONE BECAUSE OURS IS NOW THE MOST IMPORTANT RELATIONSHIP IN OUR LIVES

WHAT DOES IT REALLY MEAN TO 'LEAVE'?

Now, you must understand that leaving your parents doesn't necessarily mean you are permanently cut off from them, or you no longer have a good child-to-parent relationship with them. This is not leaving but rather isolating oneself.

In fact, the Bible says this concerning our relationship with our parents:

"Honour your father and your mother,
that your days may be long upon the land
which the LORD your God is giving you."

EXODUS 20:12 [5]

We have a duty to our parents, and that is to show respect and honour to them, and marriage must not rob us of honouring them at any time. This means you must leave them with love, respect, and admiration for their sacrifices. You must break away from them and stop relying on them. When you were with them, they were the ones giving to you. Now is the time for you to give back to them, as a responsibility of caring for them in return, even if you are away from them.

Consequently, you know and understand your parents more, and it is important to be sensitive when leaving certain types of parents.

If your parent is a single parent, where you were raised by your father or mother but not both, such a parent may not have anyone to lean on at home and feel very alone. You may have left behind a parent in a marriage that is lifeless and devoid of passion. Your departure has left a huge void at home. It's vital to express your love and dedication to them while making your spouse at home your primary priority.

Now here is the balance regarding leaving your parents. First, it is not wrong to seek your parent's advice on certain issues. In fact, seeking advice is a way you show your respect

---

5 Exodus 20: 12 (NKJV), The Holy Bible

and honour your parents. But you must let your parents know that their advice is information and not a final decision, as you will have to reach a consensus with your spouse. Also, it is very honouring to your spouse to ask for their consent, before seeking advice from parents.

On the other hand, for parents, there is nothing wrong with you desiring to gift your children or ease their finances. However, you must never see that as your usual duty, and understand they can also respectfully decline your offer.

'This means you must leave them with love, respect, and admiration for their sacrifices'.

THE DIVINE CALL TO SEVERANCE

God's design for marriage is deeply rooted in the sacred principle of severance. As two individuals come together in holy matrimony, they are called to leave behind their former lives and commit to a new life as one.

The process of severance is not merely a physical act of leaving one's parental home but a spiritual and emotional surrender, signifying a new beginning and a complete devotion to the marriage covenant. In God's wisdom, this severance is necessary to create a foundation of unity between husband and wife.

> *"...and the two shall become one flesh,*
> *so then they are no longer two, but one flesh."*
> MARK 10:8 [6]

---

6 Mark 10:8 (NKJV), The Holy Bible

And, of course, the divine purpose of marriage is to form an unbreakable bond where two souls intertwine, becoming one flesh in the eyes of the Almighty. As a Christian couple, embracing the call to severance is an act of obedience and reverence to God's plan, laying the groundwork for a flourishing and harmonious union.

IN GOD'S WISDOM, THIS SEVERANCE IS NECESSARY TO CREATE A FOUNDATION OF UNITY BETWEEN HUSBAND AND WIFE

To Leave and to Cleave

To truly understand severance, you must know what it means to leave and cleave. *Leaving signifies the act of stepping away from one's parental home, letting go of the authority and dependence that once existed.* It is a declaration of spiritual and emotional independence, allowing a couple to establish their own identity and family unit under God's guidance.

However, leaving is only the beginning. The second aspect, cleaving, is just as crucial. *Cleaving entails a deep, wholehearted commitment to one another.* It is a covenantal pledge to hold fast to each other through all circumstances, to love and cherish, and to walk hand in hand on the path set before them. In cleaving, we find the essence of unity that God desires for every marriage.

Now, I want you to consider a growing tree with its fruits on it. Nothing new grows as long as the fruits remain attached to the tree. But the moment the fruit becomes ripe and falls to the ground, a new tree generation begins to spring up. The same thing applies to marriage. You cannot remain dependent and become marriageable; that is not God's ordinance for marriage.

When a man and woman leave their parental homes and come together in marriage, their primary allegiance shifts to each other. *They become each other's confidant, support, and companion.* This prioritization allows them to grow and flourish together, leaning on God's grace to navigate the challenges and joys of married life.

I've seen many couples who haven't truly 'left' their families of origin. They're still emotionally tied to their parents and can't seem to let go. This can be especially true for women who have a close bond with their mothers, or men who rely on their fathers for financial support. Unless both partners in a marriage are committed to severing themselves from their original families and making their spouse their top priority, their marriage is unlikely to succeed.

So, if you're getting married or already married, remember to 'leave and cleave.' It might feel like a betrayal or cause you to feel guilty, but it's the best thing for your marriage and your relationship with your parents. And who knows, you might even end up loving them twice as much!

In cleaving, we find the essence of unity that God desires for every marriage.

WHEN A MAN AND WOMAN LEAVE THEIR PARENTAL HOMES AND COME TOGETHER IN MARRIAGE, THEIR PRIMARY ALLEGIANCE SHIFTS TO EACH OTHER

PARENTS WANT TO REATTACH

Often, without our knowledge, we allow our parents to reestablish their broken connections. This could happen during a visit like the festive season or a time of celebration in the home. This reattachment could happen during a telephone call when the child tells the parent about a disappointment or failure in their marriage.

Do not be quick to share your spouse's weaknesses with your parent, especially when there is conflict in the home. Many marital conflicts arise because couples fail to fully sever from their parents, leading to interference, divided loyalties, and weakened commitment.

Each time you talk down on your spouse before your parent because of an unresolved issue, you are inviting a third party into your home. When issues are resolved between your spouse and yourself, your parents will never forget, and that might, in turn, hurt your home.

It is important that you do not let your parents drive a wedge, innocently or not so innocently, between your spouse and yourself. Some parents will try to manipulate their children and control them. A father may not stop telling his daughter what to do. It is necessary for the husband to intervene and tell his wife that such behaviour can be damaging to their marriage. It may be necessary to set boundaries that limit the amount of communication between the father and daughter, either for the short or long term.

Likewise, it is possible a mother might try to dictate the terms of her son's relationship. This is not also healthy for the son's marriage. If the mother observes anything, she could try to talk with her son and not force her opinion on her son. If the situation does not improve, the husband may need to take a break from his mother. He should focus his attention on his wife.

The concept of severance is not about abandoning parents or cutting off relationships but about prioritizing the marital covenant above all other human ties. Jesus Himself emphasised this in Matthew 19:5 when He reiterated Genesis 2:24, reinforcing that *marriage requires a complete shift in allegiance.*

In modern marriages, however, many couples struggle with enmeshment – a psychological term describing overly dependent relationships with parents that hinder marital independence.

A 2024 report from the American Association for Marriage and Family Therapy (AAMFT) revealed that nearly 50% of couples in therapy cited 'lack of healthy boundaries with parents' as a recurring issue[7]. This dependency often manifests in decision-making, finances, and emotional support, where one or both spouses still seek parental approval, or intervention, rather than relying on each other. The consequences can be devastating, leading to resentment, power struggles, and even divorce.

One of the most tangible manifestations of failed severance in modern marriages is financial entanglement with parents. According to comprehensive 2023 data from the Pew Research Centre, more than one-quarter (27%) of married adults aged 18-34 continue to rely on parental financial assistance. This support most frequently goes toward two of life's most significant expenses: housing (42% of cases) and childcare (28% of cases)[8]

What begins as temporary help during challenging times often evolves into an ongoing dependency that subtly undermines marital autonomy. The psychological impact of this dynamic is profound, as documented in a 2023 Journal of Family and Economic Issues study.[9] Their research revealed that couples receiving regular financial support from parents were 1.5 times more likely to experience money-related conflicts compared to financially independent

---

7 American Association for Marriage and Family Therapy. About marriage and family therapists. AAMFT. Retrieved March 27, 2025, from https://www.aamft.org/AAMFT/About_AAMFT/About_Marriage_and_Family_Therapists.aspx

8 Pew Research Centre. (2024, January 25). Financial help and independence in young adulthood. Pew Research Centre. Retrieved from https://www.pewresearch.org/social-trends/2024/01/25/financial-help-and-independence-in-young-adulthood/

9 Mammen, K. (2020). Children's gender and investments from non-resident fathers. Journal of Family and Economic Issues, 41, 332-349.

couples. Even more telling, nearly two-thirds (65%) [10] of these couples reported feeling pressured to comply with parental expectations regarding how they should spend their money, creating an invisible third party in financial decisions that should only be resolved between spouses.

This financial umbilical cord frequently becomes a source of resentment, as it contradicts the biblical mandate for couples to establish their own independent household (Genesis 2:24).

EACH TIME YOU TALK DOWN ON YOUR SPOUSE BEFORE YOUR PARENT BECAUSE OF AN UNRESOLVED ISSUE, YOU ARE INVITING A THIRD PARTY INTO YOUR HOME

Husbands, Protect Your Wife After Severance

As the head of the family, you are to protect your home with your strength, wisdom and might as a man. You may have to step in and protect your wife from manipulative parents. I urge you to protect your wife and your marriage by gently protecting her heart from a parent whose intentions are good, but counterproductive.

You may want to consider spending less time in your hometown if you're having difficulty maintaining a clean

---

10 Monk, J. K., Bordere, T. C., & Benson, J. J. (2021). Emerging ideas. Advancing family science through public scholarship: Fostering community relationships and engaging in broader impacts. *Family Relations, 70*(5), 1612-1625.

break. Maybe the visit should only last two or three nights instead of a whole week. You can also skip the holiday to make it clear where your priority is. To avoid misunderstanding and to help you make decisions, it is important to establish your family values as early as possible in your marriage.

According to 2024 Pew Research findings, financial dependence persists well into adulthood for many Americans. The study shows that 59% of parents provide financial support to their adult children (ages 18-34). Among 18–24-year-olds, 57% live with their parents, though 75% of those receiving assistance remain optimistic about achieving future independence[11.]

These figures highlight the ongoing economic challenges that delay financial autonomy for younger generations. This dependence often leads to marital power imbalances, where parents retain influence over major decisions like home purchases, childcare, and career moves.

The failure to sever properly creates a triangular relationship dynamic, where the spouse competes with parents for influence, creating a recipe for discord.

Sometimes, your parents may require your help as they age. Give yourself as much time as possible to make important decisions with your spouse, particularly those that will have long-term consequences. In most cases, your marriage health must come first. You must also consider the financial

11 Sheidlower, N. (2024, January 27). Most parents are still giving money to their young adult kids, survey found. Business Insider Africa. Retrieved March 27, 2025, from https://africa.businessinsider.com/news/most-parents-are-still-giving-money-to-their-young-adult-kids-survey-found/b1grwmr

impact. You see, a parent might need to move into a retirement home if their presence would negatively affect your marriage.

Now, you must remember that severance isn't a one-time thing or something limited to the first years of marriage. As long as your parents are still alive, you will be tempted to reconnect old bonds. When grandchildren are born, parents will want to pass on their wealth of knowledge about raising children. Parents and children must both be on guard to ensure that the leaving is a healthy realignment in the relationship between parent and child.

Each phase in the marriage presents unique challenges to marital autonomy that require wisdom and intentionality. The biblical model remains remarkably relevant in this context – while honouring parents remains a lifelong commandment (Exodus 20:12), the priority of the marital bond never diminishes.

Severance, as the first essential element of Christian marriage, sets the stage for a covenantal union blessed by God. As we continue on our journey, we will uncover the remaining three elements of Christian marriage. Each element is interwoven with the other, forming a beautiful tapestry that represents God's divine masterpiece in marriage.

TO AVOID MISUNDERSTANDING AND TO HELP YOU MAKE DECISIONS, IT IS IMPORTANT TO ESTABLISH YOUR FAMILY VALUES AS EARLY AS POSSIBLE IN YOUR MARRIAGE

REFLECTION QUESTIONS FOR COUPLES

1. What is one way you still rely on your parents instead of your spouse?

2. How can you create healthier boundaries with extended family?

3. What steps will you take this month to prioritise your spouse?

CASE STUDY:
MICHAEL AND SARAH – THE IN-LAW INVASION

Michael and Sarah had a beautiful start to their marriage. Their wedding was a dream, their home was cosy, and their love felt unshakable. But by the second year, Sarah started to feel like she was married, not just to Michael but also to his mother. Every weekend, Michael's mom would show up unannounced, bringing home-cooked meals, reorganising their kitchen, and slipping in comments about how 'things were done right' in her day. At first, Sarah tried to be gracious. But deep down, she felt invisible in her own home.

Michael didn't understand the problem. His mom was trying to help, he reasoned. She'd always been close to him; this was just how their family expressed love. But Sarah began to withdraw. She no longer looked forward to weekends. She avoided deep conversations and started sleeping earlier to avoid confrontations. Their once-vibrant connection dimmed.

One Sunday after church, a sermon on 'Leaving and Cleaving' stirred something in Michael. He saw Sarah wiping tears during the message. That evening, they finally talked. Sarah opened up about feeling like a guest in her own marriage. She explained how much it hurt when he didn't protect their space and made her question her place in his heart.

Michael was quiet. For the first time, he realised he hadn't indeed 'left' his parents emotionally. He apologised and asked Sarah to help him set boundaries honouring his mother and marriage. They sat down together to write a message to his mom, not as a dismissal, but as a loving reminder that they were now building something new. Michael reassured his mom of her value while firmly requesting space for their growth.

In time, things began to change. Sarah felt more confident and seen. Michael became more intentional, consulting Sarah before inviting guests or seeking advice. Their weekends became their own again—sometimes spent visiting family, alone, but always as a united front.

ENCOURAGEMENT

True severance isn't about cutting off parents but prioritising the new home. When a man leaves, he opens the door for cleaving. When a wife feels protected, she blooms in trust and honour. God blesses the home where His order is respected.

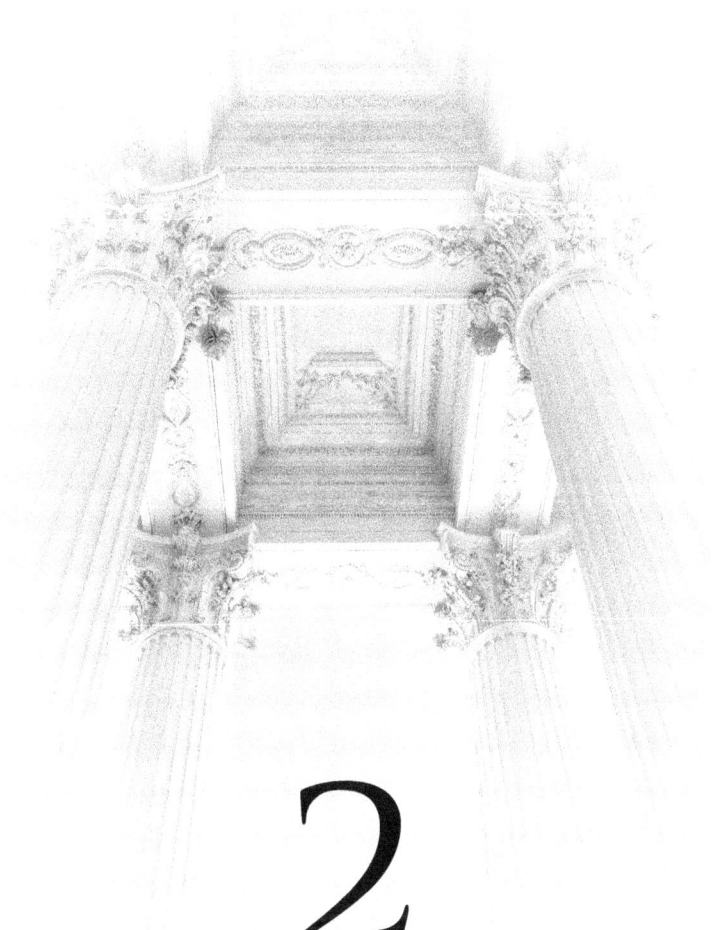

2

PERMANENCE

2

PERMANENCE

"Therefore, what God has joined together,
let not man separate."

MARK 10:9 [12]

In the Bible, God created Eve from Adam's rib (Genesis 2:22). Invariably, Eve became a part of man, and the two were inseparable because of how God fashioned his side. God has joined the two in a one-flesh permanent relationship.

Now, God had joined these two, as husband and wife, in one flesh. The couple is permanently united in a lifelong covenant relationship. And, of course, nobody has the moral or legal authority to break what God has bonded together.

---

12 Mark 10:9 (NKJV), The Holy Bible – "Therefore what God has joined together, let not man separate."

In this chapter, you will find out what the Bible says about permanence in marriage, separation in marriage and divorce.

Marriage Unbroken

"...And be joined to his wife,
and they shall become one flesh."
GENESIS 2:24B [13]

In some other Bible renditions, the word 'joined' used above, also means 'cleave' or united, which means:

+ To cling
+ To stick (or glue)
+ To hold fast
+ To glue yourself to your wife in a lasting bond

God seals the marriage of two people with a bond that can never be broken. In other words, husband and wife become 'glued' together – bound together into one unit.

Permanence is an interesting feature of glue. The same applies to people 'glued' in marriage. The marriage is permanent until death. Genesis 2:24 does not allow for divorce or remarriage. This issue is important and should not be ignored. According to God's word, the answer to divorce is obvious: marriage is permanent. When a couple makes the commitment to stay together for life, they create a sense of security, stability, and trust that can withstand the inevitable challenges that come with any long-term relationship.

---

13 Genesis 2:24 (NKJV), The Holy Bible.

Through permanence, a couple is not only making a promise to one another but also to God. They acknowledge that their marriage is not just a union between two individuals, but a covenant with God. This covenant is based on the love, honour, and respect the couple has for each other, and it reflects their desire to honour and glorify God through their marriage.

GOD SEALS THE MARRIAGE OF TWO PEOPLE WITH A BOND THAT CAN NEVER BE BROKEN

What is Permanence in Marriage?

Marriage is not a temporary agreement that can be dissolved when difficulties arise. Instead, it is a lifelong covenant established by God Himself. In a world where divorce is increasingly common, Christians must return to the biblical truth that marriage is meant to be permanent, enduring, and unbreakable, except in cases explicitly permitted by Scripture (such as sexual immorality or abandonment, as noted in Matthew 19:9) [14]

Permanence in marriage means the following:

+ A couple is willing to work through any difficulties and challenges that they may encounter

---

14 Matthew 19:9 (NKJV), The Holy Bible – "Whoever divorces his wife, except for sexual immorality, and marries another, commits adultery; and whoever marries her who is divorced commits adultery."

+ They are committed to growing and learning together
+ They will support each other through the ups and downs of life

When a couple chooses to stay together through the good times and the bad, they create a bond that is unbreakable and a love that is stronger than any obstacle.

Permanence in marriage is also a testament to the power of forgiveness. When a couple makes the commitment to stay together for life, they must be willing to forgive one another and work through any conflicts that arise. Any couple can heal past wounds and build a stronger, more loving relationship.

When it comes to the issue of permanence in marriage, it's easy to focus on the challenges and difficulties that can arise in a long-term relationship. However, it's important to remember that permanence is actually a beautiful and positive aspect of marriage that can bring tremendous joy and fulfilment to your life. One of the most powerful examples of permanence in marriage is found in the story of Adam and Eve.

Adam saw Eve for the very first time, and He could affirm that at last, this is the bone of my bones and flesh of my flesh. This one shall be called woman, for from man was she taken (Genesis 2:23). This is the level of conviction needed to start the journey of marriage, where you are a part of me, and I am part of you.

Of course, Eve was not without flaws, but Adam chose to look past her flaws and stay. There was a time Eve allowed her emotions to overrule her, by believing the lies and deceptions of the devil (Genesis 3). The devil took advantage of that weakness, but Adam, her husband, never quit their union because of her weakness.

Likewise, Adam was not without his own flaws. Adam defaulted in his leadership role by being quick to blame others for his mistakes (Genesis 3:12). Nevertheless, Eve, his wife, didn't cease to be the dearest woman to him.

You can see that although their relationship was far from perfect, they remained committed to each other through all of their trials and tribulations. This is a powerful example of what true love and commitment can look like in a marriage.

When you commit to permanence in your marriage, you are making a powerful statement about your love for your spouse. You are saying that you are willing to stick with him or her through thick and thin, no matter what life may throw your way. This type of commitment can be incredibly powerful, as it gives both you and your spouse a sense of security and stability in your relationship.

PERMANENCE IN MARRIAGE IS ALSO A TESTAMENT TO THE POWER OF FORGIVENESS

YOUR VOW

At the heart of permanence in marriage are the vows exchanged between a husband and wife. These promises are not to be taken lightly, for they are spoken in the presence of God and are binding in His sight. The act of making vows is not just a ritual; it is a sacred commitment, a solemn promise to love, honour, and cherish one another until death.

> *"Who keeps an oath even when it hurts,*
> *and does not change their mind."*
> PSALM 15:4 [15]

Permanence requires a steadfast determination to keep one's vows, even when challenges arise or sacrifices must be made. It is a testament to the power of integrity and the strength of character in a marriage.

Subsequently, permanence in marriage does not imply a stagnant or lifeless relationship. On the contrary, it calls for a proactive effort to nurture and cultivate a lifelong love that continues to grow and deepen over time.

Ephesians 4:2-3 advises us,

> *"Be completely humble and gentle; be patient,*
> *bearing with one another in love. Make*
> *every effort to keep the unity of the Spirit*
> *through the bond of peace."* [16]

---

15 Psalm 15:4 (NKJV), The Holy Bible – *"Who keeps an oath even when it hurts, and does not change their mind."*

16 Ephesians 4:2-3 (NKJV) – The Holy Bible

Permanence involves daily choices to extend grace, forgive, and seek reconciliation when conflicts arise. It means continually investing in the emotional, spiritual, and physical intimacy of the marital relationship.

PERMANENCE REQUIRES A STEADFAST DETERMINATION TO KEEP ONE'S VOWS, EVEN WHEN CHALLENGES ARISE OR SACRIFICES MUST BE MADE

ONE MAN, ONE WIFE

God gave Adam only one wife when He created him in the Garden of Eden. Adam didn't have any spare wives if he ever decided to divorce Eve, which reveals God's original intention for marriage: **one man, one wife, forever.**

When the Pharisees challenged Jesus on the issue of divorce, he referred them back to the beginning of creation to show them how God intended marriage to be (Mark 10:9, Matthew 19:6).

Jesus quoted Genesis to answer the Pharisee's question about ending marriage. They wanted to know if a man could legally get out of his marriage. Jesus knew what they were thinking.

The wrong question was being asked. He knew they were all too willing to be cruel towards their wives. They wanted to know how they could end their marriage. Jesus wanted them to see marriage in a different light. The main reason to marry was to be with each other. He cited words from the Law to remind them of the basics of marriage.

At the time that two people made their vows to be with each other, the thought of separation was far from their minds. Now, it seemed that separation had become the focal point of marital analysis. What changed?

Jesus explains it beautifully in Matthew.

> *"Consequently, they are no*
> *more two but one flesh."*
> MATTHEW 19:6 [17]

This will be discussed in more detail later when we examine 'one flesh'; however, for now, just know that Jesus was reminding them that it is prior to vows and not after them, that they can decide to leave a marriage. In marriage, you lose your unilateral right to walk out as you will. Both couples are now dependent on each other. It is better and easier to isolate the two wooden blocks before glueing them than after.

It will interest you to know that saying this does not mean that couples have no cause for divorce, as they have stuck together. Jesus replied to the Pharisees that they asked about separation, not divorce. They are not the exact same.

---

17 Matthew 19:6 (NKJV) – The Holy Bible

ADAM DIDN'T HAVE ANY SPARE WIVES IF HE EVER DECIDED TO DIVORCE EVE, WHICH REVEALS GOD'S ORIGINAL INTENTION FOR MARRIAGE: ONE MAN, ONE WIFE, FOREVER

Commitment in Marriage

Divorce, which does not reflect the couple's true status before God, is always wrong. Remarriage (except for widows or widowers) is adultery because it brings partners together, who do not have the right to be together, in God's eyes.

The 'glue' in marriage does not imply that permanence is an essential or intrinsic ingredient. It is true that the term 'cleaving' to God was used by Israel, but it was a commitment that was supposed to be permanent. The Israelites' continued adultery shows that their act of cleaving was not permanent. It is not because Israel was devoted to God that the relationship between God and Israel is permanent. This teaches us that cleaving can be a permanent bond or not.

Couples who divorce lose their right to be true to their vow of companionship, making divorce a poison to marital unions.

However, you could have reasons to justify divorce as the best option in the situation of adultery. But before you make your conclusion, I want you to consider the marriage of prophet Hosea and Gomer (Hosea 1:2-3).

In Hosea 1:2, the Bible says;

> *"The LORD said to Hosea,*
> *'Go, take to yourself a wife of whoredom*
> *and have children of whoredom."* [18]

Hosea obeyed, marrying a woman named Gomer, who was unfaithful to him. But why did God tell Hosea to marry a prostitute?

The marriage is a result of divine instruction and conviction, just like any other marriage. Hosea's knowing Gomer was a harlot does not negate this fact. Despite Gomer's infidelity, Hosea remained committed to her and continued to love her unconditionally.

You see, God always wants to speak to the world through a home built on His instruction. God wanted to provide an illustration of His love through the marriage of Hosea to Gomer, for the people of Israel, who had been unfaithful to Him by practising idolatry. This story reminds us that even in the face of great difficulty and pain, it's possible to remain committed to our spouse and to love them with a Christ-like love, because it is God's instruction, and marriage is God's institution on earth.

> *"Then the Lord said to me, 'Go again, love a*
> *woman who is loved by a lover and is committing*
> *adultery, just like the love of the Lord for the*
> *children of Israel, who look to other gods and*
> *love the raisin cakes of the pagans. So I bought*

---

18 Hosea 1:2 (NKJV) – The Holy Bible

*her for myself for fifteen shekels of silver
and one and one-half homers of barley".*

HOSEA 3:1-2 [19]

The fact that God had to command Hosea to find Gomer and buy her back is a strong indication of the level of love, commitment, grace, and forgiveness. This is the covenant of oneness in marriage that should be kept. A covenant of marriage based on the covenant God has made with us. It is in the power of His promise to mankind that we, too, can keep our covenant in marriage against the forces that would destroy homes and ruin lives.

Likewise, the story of Joseph and Mary is a powerful reminder of the importance of permanence in marriage. Even in the face of great uncertainty and fear, Joseph chose to trust in God's plan and to remain committed to Mary (Matthew 1:19-21).

When we commit to permanence in our marriage, we are not only committing to our spouse, but we are also committing to God and His plan for our lives. This type of commitment can be incredibly powerful, as it allows you to build a deep and meaningful relationship with your spouse that is rooted in faith and trust.

A COVENANT OF MARRIAGE BASED ON THE COVENANT GOD HAS MADE WITH US

---

19 Hosea 3:1-2 (NKJV) – The Holy Bible

Separation, not Divorce

The concept of permanence in Christian marriage is not a mere suggestion or optional feature; it is an intrinsic aspect of the covenantal union established by God.

When a man and woman stand before God, their families, and their community to exchange vows of love and commitment, they are entering into a covenant that is intended to last a lifetime. Permanence is a reflection of God's unchanging nature.

In Malachi 3:6, God declares[20], *"I the LORD, do not change."* Just as God's faithfulness and love for His people remain constant, so should the love and commitment between spouses endure through the highs and lows of life.

The secular world often presents a different perspective, promoting a throwaway culture where relationships are discarded at the first sign of difficulty. But Christian marriage is built on a different foundation, one that embraces the sanctity of permanence and the transformative power of covenantal love.

In the sacred covenant of marriage, the Bible emphasises the sanctity and permanence of the union between a man and a woman. Divorce is not the ideal outcome in Christian marriage, but there are rare instances where biblical separation is recommended over divorce, and it is always with the intention of reconciliation.

---

20 Malachi 3:6 (NKJV), The Holy Bible – "For I am the Lord, I do not change; Therefore you are not consumed, O sons of Jacob."

The Bible says;

"To the married, I give this command (not I, but the Lord): A wife must not separate from her husband. But if she does, she must remain unmarried or else be reconciled to her husband. And a husband must not divorce his wife."

I CORINTHIANS 7:10-11 [21]

The wisdom of the scripture, in using words correctly at each instance, shows God's intentionality in the message being communicated. In the above scripture, the word 'separate' and 'divorce' was used differently to convey a different meaning.

Despite God's clear design, modern society often treats marriage as a temporary arrangement, rather than a lifelong covenant. According to the American Psychological Association (APA), 40-50% of first marriages in the U.S. end in divorce.

The divorce rate for second marriages is even higher (60-67%)[22], and third marriages fail at a rate of 73-74% (National Marriage Project)[23]. This trend shows that many people enter marriage with an exit strategy rather than a commitment to permanence.

21 1 Corinthians 7:10-11 (NKJV) - The Holy Bible

22 American Psychological Association. (2013, April). Can this marriage be saved? Monitor on Psychology, 44(4). Retrieved from https://www.apa.org/monitor/2013/04/marriage

23 Forbes Advisor. Revealing Divorce Statistics In 2025. Forbes. Retrieved March 27, 2025, from https://www.forbes.com/advisor/legal/divorce/divorce-statistics/

The Bible outrightly spoke about the wisdom of seeking a brief time of space to later regroup, gain perspective, and seek the Lord in times of marital challenges.

Of course, divorce is not God's desire, but if a separation occurs, it should be approached with the intention of reconciliation rather than permanent dissolution. The emphasis is on preserving the marriage bond and seeking the path of restoration.

> *"For I hate divorce!" says the LORD,*
> *the God of Israel. "To divorce your wife*
> *is to overwhelm her with cruelty," says*
> *the LORD of Heaven's Armies. "So guard*
> *your heart; do not be unfaithful to your wife."*
> MALACHI 2:16 (NLT) [24]

Subsequently, the Bible in Malachi 2:16 expresses God's hatred for divorce, emphasising the pain and harm it causes to the individuals involved. Jesus reinforced this message in his teachings (Matthew 5:31-32; 19:3-9) by stating that divorce was allowed in the Mosaic law due to the hardness of people's hearts, but it was not part of God's original plan.

When a couple faces separation, the Bible suggests that they remain unmarried or be reconciled. This implies that during the separation period, they are not free to marry someone else. The focus is on spiritual growth, seeking God's guidance, and striving for reconciliation with one's spouse.

---

24 Malachi 2:16 (NLT) – The Holy Bible

You can see throughout the Bible that God showed us instances of separation and reconciliation that offer valuable insights into the scope of permanence in marriage. One such example is the story of Hosea and Gomer.

Hosea's unfaithful wife, Gomer, abandoned him, but Hosea continued to love her and pursued her, representing God's relentless love for His people even in their unfaithfulness (Hosea 3:1-3).

Another example is the parable of the prodigal son, where the father patiently waited for his wayward son to return, and the father still embraced him in loving kindness (Luke 15:11-32). This demonstrates God's unwavering love and desire for reconciliation, even in marriage.

Marriage can be fraught with challenges, and during difficult times, a brief period of separation may allow individuals to regroup, gain perspective, and seek God for guidance. It is crucial to approach this decision prayerfully and with the intention of restoration, not escape.

My counsel to those going through a hard time that is somehow affecting the permanence of the home is that you should seek God. Seeking guidance from experienced Christian marriage counsellors and pastoral leaders can be invaluable. They can provide spiritual insight, biblical wisdom, and practical advice to navigate through the difficulties and foster reconciliation.

More so, forgiveness and grace are central to the Christian faith and play a vital role in the process of reconciliation.

Both partners must be willing to extend forgiveness and grace to each other, just as God has forgiven us through Christ (Ephesians 4:32).

In acknowledging the reality of human imperfection, it is essential to recognise that no marriage is without its struggles. However, the permanence of marriage does not demand perfection but calls for a willingness to extend grace and seek redemption.

God's grace is transformative and empowers couples to overcome challenges, heal wounds, and rebuild trust. It opens the door to a fresh start and new beginnings. Permanence is not about clinging to a toxic relationship but about embracing the potential for growth and healing through the work of God's Spirit.

John and Mary (names changed for privacy) had been married for 12 years when financial struggles nearly destroyed their relationship. After John lost his job, the stress led to constant arguments, emotional distance, and even thoughts of divorce. At their lowest moment, Mary suggested separation, believing divorce was the only way out. However, a Christian friend encouraged them to seek biblical marriage counselling before making a final decision.

Through counselling, John and Mary implemented practical changes that transformed their marriage. First, they committed to weekly prayer and budgeting sessions, setting aside dedicated time to seek God's guidance and carefully manage their finances together. This discipline helped them replace anxiety with faith and arguments with cooperation. Second, they joined a marriage-small-group at their church, which provided much-needed accountability, encouragement from older couples, and biblical wisdom for navigating challenges.

Over time, these intentional steps produced remarkable results: within two years, not only did their financial situation stabilise, but their marriage emerged stronger than ever, rekindling emotional intimacy and deepening their mutual respect.

You see, marriage challenges are an opportunity for spiritual growth and drawing closer to God, individually and as a couple, as we trust in His plans for our lives and relationships. Let us, as Christian couples, strive to uphold the sanctity of Marriage and seek reconciliation through faith, love, and the power of God's word.

Remember, God's heart is for reconciliation and restoration, and while the path may be difficult, with Him at the centre of your marriage, there is hope for healing and renewed love. Trust in His guidance and seek the support of fellow believers and wise counsellors. God bless you on your journey of reconciliation and growth in your marriage.

"GOD'S GRACE IS TRANSFORMATIVE AND EMPOWERS COUPLES TO OVERCOME CHALLENGES, HEAL WOUNDS, AND REBUILD TRUST"

The Role of Community

The permanence of marriage is not solely the responsibility of the couple themselves. The support and encouragement of a faith community are vital in upholding and strengthening the marital bond.

In Hebrews 10:24-25, we are exhorted to 'spur one another on toward love and good deeds, not giving up meeting together, as some are in the habit of doing, but encouraging one another.' Surrounding oneself with like-minded believers who prioritise permanence in Marriage creates a supportive environment where couples can find wisdom, accountability, and prayerful guidance.

Persevering in Difficult Times

Permanence is tested during times of adversity and trials. Difficult circumstances, such as financial hardships, loss of a loved one, or health challenges, can strain the marital bond. Yet, it is precisely in these moments that the power of permanence shines the brightest.

Permanence is not just about surviving challenges but also about celebrating milestones. It is about cherishing the anniversaries, the victories, and the shared memories that weave the fabric of a rich and meaningful marriage.

When a couple reflects on their journey together and the faithfulness of God throughout the years, it deepens their appreciation for the permanence of their union. Every anniversary becomes a testament to God's faithfulness and a reminder of the promise they made to each other and to Him.

Couples who embrace permanence in their marriage get a glimpse into the love and commitment God has for his people. Their union is a reflection of the covenant that Christ made with His Church. They are united in love forever, empowered to overcome challenges with grace, hope and perseverance.

To cultivate a love that lasts a lifetime, couples must make daily decisions and prioritise intimacy and unity. This will now lead us to the next most important element of marriage: UNITY.

TO CULTIVATE A LOVE THAT LASTS A LIFETIME, COUPLES MUST MAKE DAILY DECISIONS AND PRIORITISE INTIMACY AND UNITY

REFLECTION QUESTIONS FOR COUPLES

1. When have you considered giving up? What helped you stay?

2. How do you define 'commitment' in your marriage?

3. What action can you take to strengthen the long-term vision for your relationship?

CASE STUDY:
JAMES AND LILLIAN – THE SILENT GOODBYE

Twelve years of marriage. Three children. One house. A thousand arguments—and growing silence.

James and Lillian weren't enemies but weren't friends anymore. Life had become routine: wake up, get the kids ready, go to work, make dinner, watch TV in silence, go to bed. Intimacy was a distant memory, replaced by frustration and unmet expectations. James had lost his job the previous year, and though he'd picked up small contracts, the loss of identity weighed heavily on him. He felt like a failure. Lillian, meanwhile, carried the weight of both parent and provider. Resentment brewed quietly.

One night, after a heated argument over a missed bill payment, Lillian packed a bag and moved to the guest room. She didn't want a divorce—yet—but she was sure they couldn't go on like this.

God, however, wasn't done with them.

A friend from their church invited them to a couples' Bible study. It felt awkward at first—two people barely spoke, trying to pretend all was well. But then they heard another couple share a similar story. Something clicked. After the session, they agreed to try again—but this time, with help.

They started counselling. They began praying together—simple, short prayers at first, then deeper, more vulnerable ones. James began to share his fears. Lillian confessed her loneliness. They cried. They fought. But they kept showing up.

Separation, as described in 1 Corinthians 7, became a tool for healing—not an escape hatch. During their brief physical and emotional space, they both sought God sincerely. And in seeking Him, they found each other again.

Today, James and Lillian say their greatest miracle wasn't avoiding divorce but rediscovering their vows. They now speak at marriage events, reminding couples that God can restore what seems dead.

ENCOURAGEMENT

Permanence doesn't mean perfection. It means persistence. It's not about avoiding hard times but choosing to stand firm in them. With God in the centre, even dry bones can rise again.

3

UNITY

3

UNITY

*For, in fact, the body is not
one member but many.*

I CORINTHIANS 12:14 [25]

Marriage is the one and only way God designed a man and his wife to become one flesh. Unity is not merely a choice but a divine calling in Christian marriage. Through unity in the home, we embrace one of the fundamental elements of our marital relationship and align ourselves with God's design and His purpose for marriage.

Truthfully, the journey of unity might not always be easy, but with Christ at the centre of our union, we can navigate through challenges, grow together, and become a powerful

---

25 1 Corinthians 12:14 (NKJV), The Holy Bible – "For in fact, the body is not one member but many."

witness to the world of God's love and grace through our marriage.

"MARRIAGE IS THE ONE AND ONLY WAY GOD DESIGNED A MAN AND HIS WIFE TO BECOME ONE FLESH"

A Love Story Rooted in Unity

One of the most inspiring examples of unity in marriage is found in the story of Ruth and Boaz (Ruth 1-4). Ruth, a young widow from Moab, was an outsider in Israel.

However, her faithfulness and love for her mother-in-law Naomi, led her to cross cultural boundaries and seek God's provision in a new land. Boaz, a wealthy and honourable man, saw Ruth's heart and character and was moved to show her kindness and compassion. Through their union, Ruth and Boaz became an integral part of God's redemptive plan, as their great-grandson would be King David and ultimately, Jesus Christ.

Interestingly, Ruth's famous declaration of unity in marriage is a testament to their deep connection when she said:

> *"Where you go, I will go, and where you stay, I will stay. Your people will be my people, and your God my God."*
> RUTH 1:16 [26]

---

26 Ruth 1:16 (NKJV), The Holy Bible – "Where you go, I will go, and where you stay, I will stay. Your people will be my people, and your God my God."

Ruth's decision to leave her homeland and embrace Naomi's God and people reflected her willingness to embrace a new identity and culture. In marriage, unity often involves navigating cultural, familial, and societal differences, choosing to cherish and respect each other's backgrounds while forging a shared identity.

God's design for unity in Christian marriage celebrates the diversity found within the union. Just as the body of Christ is composed of various parts, each with its unique function (1 Corinthians 12:12) [27], so too is a marriage enriched by the diversity of its partners. Learning to embrace and appreciate these differences creates a vibrant and dynamic relationship, where both partners contribute their strengths for the greater good of the marriage.

Something interesting about the marriage between Ruth and Boaz is that it transcends beyond them. This marriage played a vital role in God's redemptive plan for humanity.

Amazingly, this has always been God's intention that every home coming together will bear fruit beyond them, into many generations, after them. Hence, the reason the devil always attacks the home.

You see, Ruth and Boaz's obedience to God's leading and their commitment to each other demonstrate the transformative power of unity and how God can use a unified couple to bring about His purposes on earth.

---

27 1 Corinthians 12:12 (NKJV), The Holy Bible – "For as the body is one and has many members, but all the members of that one body, being many, are one body, so also is Christ."

GOD'S DESIGN FOR UNITY IN CHRISTIAN MARRIAGE CELEBRATES THE DIVERSITY FOUND WITHIN THE UNION

ONENESS IN THE HOME

The story of Peter and Jane illustrates how contrasting backgrounds can strain a marriage. Peter, raised in a strict, schedule-driven home, clashed with Jane's spontaneous, free-spirited nature. Small disagreements—like mealtimes or spending habits—escalated into recurring arguments. Studies show that if unresolved, 69% of these early conflicts persist, eroding marital satisfaction over time (Gottman Institute, 2019).[28]

However, their turning point came when they stopped viewing their differences as obstacles and instead as complementary strengths. Through open communication and compromise, they learned that unity doesn't mean thinking alike—it means working together toward common goals.

Subsequently, when God created Eve from Adam's rib, He brought together two individuals who were designed to complement each other perfectly. Adam recognized the unity and oneness that God had created in their relationship, declaring;

---

28 Gottman Institute. Marriage and Couples. The Gottman Institute. Retrieved March 27, 2025, from https://www.gottman.com/about/research/couples/

"This is now bone of my bones and flesh
of my flesh; she shall be called 'woman,'
for she was taken out of man"
GENESIS 2:23 [29]

Through their union, Adam and Eve were able to fulfil God's command to be fruitful and multiply and to exercise dominion over the earth. Unity brings possibility. Any home that seems divided will achieve little or no result.

When a husband and wife are united, they can work together to overcome any obstacle that comes their way. A home that is divided, on the other hand, will achieve little or no result.

In a Christian marriage, unity means being of one mind and heart. It means working together towards a common goal, which is to glorify God and to love and serve one another. This unity is not just a physical union but a spiritual one as well. It requires a deep commitment to each other and to God.

When a couple is united in their marriage, they can accomplish great things. They can raise a family that loves and honours God. They can serve their community and make a positive impact on the world. They can weather any storm and overcome any challenge that comes their way.

On the other hand, a divided home will struggle to accomplish anything. When a husband and wife are not on

---

29 Genesis 2:23 (NKJV), The Holy Bible – "This is now bone of my bones and flesh of my flesh; she shall be called 'woman,' for she was taken out of man."

the same page, they will work against each other, instead of working together. This can lead to conflict, stress, and tension, which can affect every area of their lives.

> *"Two are better than one because they*
> *have a good return for their labour:*
> *If either of them falls down, one can*
> *help the other up. But pity anyone who*
> *falls and has no one to help them up. Also,*
> *if two lie down together, they will keep warm.*
> *But how can one keep warm alone?"*
> ECCLESIASTES 4:9-11 [30]

The book of Ecclesiastes offers insights into the importance of unity in marriage. The above passage reminds us that unity in marriage is not just a matter of emotion or feeling, but of practicality and support.

The best marriages are those in which both partners maintain their individuality and goals while working together to bring about God's rule in and through their union.

Unrealistic expectations can lead to disappointment in the future, for some couples, when they get married. Couples are more likely to be consumed by their marriage than compelled to greatness if they do not protect and respect each other's unique identities, purposes, talents, skills, and callings.

The truth is, spending quality time together is essential in fostering unity and oneness in the home. Pursuing shared

---

30 Ecclesiastes 4:9-11 (NKJV), The Holy Bible

hobbies and interests provides opportunities for couples to connect emotionally, mentally, and even spiritually.

Learn to engage in activities you both enjoy together, as this enhances unity beyond the marital relationship. Be your partner's best friend and biggest cheerleader.

ANY HOME THAT SEEMS DIVIDED WILL ACHIEVE LITTLE OR NO RESULT

Christ and the Church – A Model for Unity

"Therefore a man shall leave his father and mother and hold fast to his wife, and the two shall become one flesh. This mystery is profound, and I am saying that it refers to Christ and the church."
EPHESIANS 5:31-32 [31]

The unity displayed in the relationship between Christ and the Church serves as the ultimate model for Christian marriage. In Ephesians 5:31-32, the apostle Paul draws a parallel between the marital union and the spiritual union between Christ and His followers:

Christian couples are called to reflect this spiritual oneness in their marriage. Just as Christ cherishes, loves, and sacrifices for His Church, husbands are called to love their wives sacrificially (Ephesians 5:25).

---

31 Ephesians 5:31-32 (NKJV), The Holy Bible

In doing so, they demonstrate the essence of unity within marriage.

IDENTITY AND UNITY

"The goal in marriage is not to think alike but to think together."
ROBERT DODD [32]

One common misconception about unity in marriage is that it involves becoming identical to one's spouse, losing one's individuality in the process.

However, God's design for unity is more profound and beautiful. Christian marriage celebrates the uniqueness of each partner while forging a deep and unbreakable bond between them.

"As each has received a gift, use it to serve one another as good stewards of God's varied grace"
I PETER 4:10 [33]

Each partner brings unique gifts, talents, and perspectives to the marriage, enriching the relationship and glorifying God through their individuality.

The healthiest marriage is the one in which both parties maintain their identities and purposes while working together in unity to fulfil God's purpose in and through their partnership.

---

32 Dodds, R. C. The goal in marriage is not to think alike, but to think together. Marriage.com. Retrieved from https://www.marriage.com/quotes/4

33 1 Peter 4:10 (NKJV), The Holy Bible – "As each has received a gift, use it to serve one another, as good stewards of God's varied grace."

The most difficult thing about being married is figuring out how to keep your sense of self, preferences, and boundaries intact. You might not even be aware of it. It's easy to forget who you are when so much of your life intersects with another person.

To best serve your unity in marriage, you must first and foremost preserve your individuality. It is possible to have a greater impact on God's kingdom by combining the strengths, minds, and spirits of two people who are steadfast in their faith in Him, and in His plan for their lives.

The work of preservation is the most important thing we can do to keep our marriages together. We need to activate our spiritual monitoring system to get a clear picture of our marriage's atmosphere. What spiritual gauge, then, can we use to measure unity in marriage?

"I, therefore, the prisoner of the Lord,
beseech you to walk worthy of the calling
with which you were called, with all
lowliness and gentleness, with longsuffering,
bearing with one another in love."
EPHESIANS 4:1-2 [34]

The unity in marriage is characterised by:

+ Humility
+ Gentleness
+ Patience
+ Tolerance in love

---

34 Ephesians 4:1-2 (NKJV), The Holy Bible

Let's take a look at how these virtues work to cultivate the spirit of unity in marriages.

TO BEST SERVE YOUR UNITY IN MARRIAGE, YOU MUST FIRST AND FOREMOST PRESERVE YOUR INDIVIDUALITY

HUMILITY IN MARRIAGE

Are you willing to submit your desires, no matter how good they may be, to God's plan for your marriage for the sake of unity? Are you willing to put your partner's needs ahead of your own, even at the expense of your own? (Philippians 2:3–4).

Humility is the virtue that enables us to submit our desires, ambitions, and egos to God's plan for our marriage. It requires a selfless attitude, where we prioritise our partner's needs above our own, even when it comes at a personal cost. As we embrace humility in our marriage, we cultivate an environment where unity can flourish and God's love can abound.

But you must understand that humility begins with a willingness to submit your own desires and plans to God's will for your marriage. It involves recognising that God's design for your relationship is far greater and more fulfilling than any plans you may have concocted for yourself.

Furthermore, the Bible says;

> *Do nothing out of selfish ambition*
> *or vain conceit. Rather, in humility,*
> *value others above yourselves, not looking*
> *to your own interests but each of you to*
> *the interests of the others.*
> PHILIPPIANS 2:3-4 (NIV)[35]

The above Biblical principle is especially relevant in marriage. Humility prompts us to prioritise our partner's needs, preferences, and well-being, even above our own. It calls us to be attentive and sensitive to their feelings, desires, and aspirations, fostering an environment of mutual respect and care.

GENTLENESS

The word 'gentleness' may evoke different connotations for different individuals, but in the context of Christian marriage, it embodies a spirit of grace, kindness, and compassion towards your spouse. Gentleness is the antithesis of reacting with anger, harshness, or bitterness when faced with challenges or conflicts within the marriage.

In any relationship, there will be moments when disagreements and conflicts arise. These moments can often be testing grounds for the virtue of gentleness. It is easy to let our emotions take the lead, responding with anger or defensiveness, especially when we feel wronged or misunderstood by our

---

35 Philippians 2:3-4 (NIV), The Holy Bible – "Do nothing out of selfish ambition or vain conceit. Rather, in humility value others above yourselves, not looking to your own interests but each of you to the interests of the others."

partner. However, such reactions can be like thorns in the flesh, causing pain and division in the marriage.

Are you a thorn in the flesh to your partner? In the face of opposition, do you find yourself reacting angrily? What is your first, unfiltered reaction if your mate wrongs you?

The Bible says:

> *"Therefore, as God's chosen people,*
> *holy and dearly loved, clothe yourselves*
> *with compassion, kindness, humility,*
> *gentleness and patience."*
> COLOSSIANS 3:12 (NIV)[36]

This gentleness is not a weakness but a manifestation of Christ's strength in our lives, empowering us to respond with grace and love even in challenging situations.

You see, when we respond to our partner's wrongs with gentleness, we demonstrate the transformative power of Christ's love. Just as Christ forgave us and extended grace to us, we, too, can offer that same grace to our spouse. In doing so, we create an environment of safety, vulnerability, and trust in the marriage.

Gentleness acts as a powerful catalyst in breaking the cycle of anger and bitterness that can plague relationships. When one spouse chooses gentleness, it disarms the potential for further conflict and opens the door for healthy communication and reconciliation.

---

36 Colossians 3:12 (NIV), The Holy Bible

IT REQUIRES A SELFLESS ATTITUDE, WHERE WE PRIORITISE OUR PARTNER'S NEEDS ABOVE OUR OWN, EVEN WHEN IT COMES AT A PERSONAL COST

PATIENCE

Waiting for God's work in your partner's life through His Spirit is a big step. Is your partner's life-changing too slowly for your liking? Do you have the patience to wait for your spouse's discernment and the guidance of the Holy Spirit before making a change?

Patience is a virtue often tested and refined in the context of marriage. As spouses, we may find ourselves eagerly desiring growth and change in our partner's life, yet God's work in their hearts may seem slow by our standards. Patience in marriage involves waiting on God's timing and trusting in His transformative work through the Holy Spirit.

It is natural to desire positive changes in our partner's life, especially when we see areas where growth and improvement are needed. However, impatience can lead to frustration, pressure, and even conflict in the marriage. We may be tempted to take matters into our own hands, attempting to force change or impose our will on our spouse.

While waiting for change, we are called to love our spouse unconditionally. This love is not based on their performance, or the speed of their growth but on the knowledge that they are God's beloved child. Love enables us to be patient, gracious, and supportive, even in the midst of challenges.

TOLERANCE IN LOVE

Do you have difficulty in making things go as you want them to? Do you accept the variety of ways in which the Holy Spirit manifests Himself in other people? Do you get along with your partner even if your personal preferences differ from theirs?

You see, each one of these indicators threatens unity in marriages. Your marriage monitoring system should activate some unity preservation practices to counteract the threat when your marriage is under attack.

> *"Do nothing from selfish ambition*
> *or conceit, but in humility count others*
> *more significant than yourselves. Let each*
> *of you look not only to his own interests*
> *but also to the interests of others."*
> PHILIPPIANS 2:3-4 [37]

At the core of unity in Christian marriage is selfless love. Selfless love is a love that puts the needs and desires of one's spouse above one's own.

In the same vein, 1 Corinthians 13:4-7 provides a profound description of love:

---

37 Philippians 2:3-4 (NKJV), The Holy Bible

"Love is patient and kind; love does not envy or boast; it is not arrogant or rude. It does not insist on its own way; it is not irritable or resentful; it does not rejoice at wrongdoing but rejoices with the truth. Love bears all things, believes all things, hopes all things, endures all things." [38]

Truthfully, an attitude of love is required for unity to be found in a marriage. Ask yourself, 'Will sharing my feelings bring me closer to my spouse?' Repression of strong feelings and beliefs can widen the social, emotional, and psychological distance between two people in a romantic relationship.

Subsequently, Jesus exemplified sacrificial love when He laid down His life for humanity. In Ephesians 5:2, we are encouraged to 'walk in love, as Christ loved us and gave himself up for us, a fragrant offering and sacrifice to God.' Similarly, in marriage, both partners are called to sacrificially love one another.

This sacrificial love manifests itself in various ways. It means:

+ Putting aside personal ambitions to support the dreams and aspirations of one's spouse

+ Choosing forgiveness instead of holding onto grudges

+ Seeking reconciliation and understanding instead of insisting on being right

---

38 1 Corinthians 13:4-7 (NKJV), The Holy Bible

Sacrifice is the essence of love, and it fosters unity by creating an atmosphere of trust and mutual care.

AT THE CORE OF UNITY IN CHRISTIAN MARRIAGE IS SELFLESS LOVE

Honest and Open Communication Foster Unity

"Speak the truth in love."

EPHESIANS 4:15 [39]

To foster unity in marriage, it is not just about what you say but how you say it. Effective communication is vital in fostering unity within a Christian marriage. Communication based on truth and love strengthens the marital bond, as it promotes transparency and vulnerability between partners.

Clear and honest communication serves as a tool for resolving conflicts and misunderstandings. When partners freely share their thoughts, feelings, and concerns, they create an environment where unity can flourish.

To truly unite as a couple, it is essential to be open and honest about one's feelings, needs, thoughts, and beliefs with one's spouse. Keeping a long list of personal grievances and secretly harbouring resentment are not the best ways to build a strong marriage.

---

39 Ephesians 4:15 (NKJV), The Holy Bible

For fear of hurting your partner's feelings or getting caught up in a fight, husbands and wives often become reluctant to express their true feelings about various issues.

However, the Bible says;

> *"There is no fear in love,*
> *but perfect love casts out fear."*
> I JOHN 4:18 [40]

Always speak the truth in love, and never have the mind to hurt your partner with your words. Both of you will emerge stronger together and quickly resolve conflicts when you express your feelings with your spouse. Even when your partner is expressing disappointment, discouragement, and anger, you can emerge stronger from the experience.

Sharing one's feelings and emotions is crucial, but how one does so is equally important. Partners should express their feelings in a sensitive, open, and kind way, allowing for easy responses from each other without exploding in anger or assuming a self-righteous air.

Furthermore, communication is not merely about expressing oneself but also about actively listening to one's spouse. James 1:19 advises:

> *"Let every person be quick to hear,*
> *slow to speak, slow to anger."* [41]

---

40 1 John 4:18 (NKJV), The Holy Bible

41 James 1:19 (NKJV), The Holy Bible

Active listening involves giving undivided attention to one's partner, seeking to understand their perspective without interruption or judgment. Likewise, show empathy. Empathy is an integral part of active listening.

Empathising with your spouse means putting oneself in their shoes, acknowledging their emotions, and validating their experiences. This level of understanding builds emotional intimacy and strengthens the bond between spouses.

ALWAYS SPEAK THE TRUTH IN LOVE, AND NEVER HAVE THE MIND TO HURT YOUR PARTNER WITH YOUR WORDS

DEVELOPING A COMMON GROUND OF THOUGHT

"Fulfill my joy by being like-minded, having the same love, being of one accord, of one mind."
PHILIPPIANS 2:2 [42]

The Apostle Paul's advice to the Philippians is helpful in developing greater spiritual and intellectual intimacy in marriage.

Marriages between people of the same faith and doctrinal beliefs have long been recommended for believers. It is extremely difficult to achieve marital happiness and unity when couples are not in agreement on the most important aspects of life.

---

42 Philippians 2:2 (NKJV), The Holy Bible

The more righteous a person becomes, the better qualified they are to love and make others happy. While a wicked man may show little affection for his wife, a righteous man, who is filled with God's love, is sure to display this heavenly quality in all of his thoughts, feelings, words, and deeds. He will radiate love, joy, and innocence through his entire face and in every expression.

Love breeds love, joy spreads joy, and these heavenly-born emotions will continue to grow until they are perfected and glorified to the fullest extent of eternal love itself.

As couples, always learn to do everything in unity and agreement and let God's word direct you.

DEALING WITH THE THREAT OF UNITY IN MARRIAGES

"So if you are offering your gift at
the altar and there, remember that your
brother has something against you; leave
your gift there before the altar and go.
First, be reconciled to your brother,
and then come and offer your gift."
MATTHEW 5:23-24 [43]

Conflict is an inevitable part of any relationship, including marriage. However, the way conflicts are handled significantly impacts the unity of a Christian marriage.

---

43 Matthew 5:23-24 (NKJV), The Holy Bible

Resolving conflicts with grace and humility allows spouses to work through their differences and grow together. It opens the door for healing, forgiveness, and reconciliation.

But the question still remains: What is the root cause of conflict in marriages?

The simple answer is when you put your own agenda ahead of God's plan for your marriage and that of your spouse. This is a selfish desire that kills the togetherness in many homes.

We all have a tendency to put our own interests ahead of those of our spouses, especially when we're married. Those who are willing to submit to the reality of God's work through the Holy Spirit are reflected in the aforementioned indicators. To what extent do each of you – individually and collectively – possess the qualities of humble submission to God's will and agenda for your home?

Forgiveness is a fundamental aspect of Christian faith, and it holds particular significance within marriage. Just as God forgives us through Christ's sacrifice, we are called to extend forgiveness to our spouses. Unresolved conflicts and unforgiveness can create barriers that hinder the unity of a marriage.

On the other hand, forgiveness liberates both parties from the weight of past mistakes and opens the door for reconciliation, leading to a stronger and more intimate connection.

THE MORE RIGHTEOUS A PERSON BECOMES, THE BETTER QUALIFIED THEY ARE TO LOVE AND MAKE OTHERS HAPPY

SEEK GOD TOGETHER

Prayer is a powerful tool for maintaining unity in Christian marriage. Couples who pray together stay together. Through your prayers, you invite God's presence into your relationship, finding strength and guidance in His wisdom.

Matthew 18:19-20 assures us saying;

> *"Again, I say to you, if two of you agree*
> *on earth about anything they ask, it will*
> *be done for them by my Father in heaven.*
> *For where two or three are gathered in*
> *my name, there am I among them."* [44]

Restoring unity requires practical steps. First, prioritise daily communication – even 10 minutes of undistracted conversation strengthens connection. Also, pray together, as couples who share spiritual practices are less likely to divorce (Stanton, 2018) [45]

---

44 Matthew 18:19-20 (NKJV), The Holy Bible

45 Stanton, G. (2018). Does faith reduce divorce risk? The Public Discourse. Retrieved from https://www.thepublicdiscourse.com/2018/03/20935/

Most recently, research conducted at Harvard's School of Public Health reveals that regularly attending church services together reduces a couple's risk of divorce by a remarkable 47% [46]. Praying together fosters unity in spirit and draws couples closer to God and each other. It aligns their hearts and desires with God's will, creating a strong spiritual foundation for the marriage.

When couples pray together and seek God's guidance, they discover a shared sense of purpose within their marriage.

*"Do two walk together unless
they have agreed to meet?"*
AMOS 3:3 [47]

Prayer aligns both partners' spiritual goals, fostering a sense of unity in their journey through life together. Shared spiritual purpose extends beyond the couple's relationship and encompasses their mission in God's kingdom. When couples unite in serving God together, their love deepens, and their marriage becomes a powerful witness to others.

PRAYER ALIGNS BOTH PARTNERS' SPIRITUAL GOALS, FOSTERING A SENSE OF UNITY IN THEIR JOURNEY THROUGH LIFE TOGETHER

46 Human Flourishing Programme at Harvard University. (2018). Religious service attendance, divorce, and remarriage among U.S. nurses in mid – and late-life. Retrieved from https://hfh.fas.harvard.edu/news/human-flourishing-program-releases-new-study-divorce

47 Amos 3:3 (NKJV), The Holy Bible

THE POWER OF SHARED RITUALS
IN BUILDING UNITY

Daily habits and traditions play a surprising role in marital unity. Research from the University of Virginia shows that couples who maintain at least three consistent rituals (like weekly date nights or morning coffee together) report to have higher satisfaction in their relationships [48] (Wilcox & Dew, 2023). These small but meaningful routines create anchors of connection amidst life's chaos.

For Peter and Jane, establishing a 'no-phones-after-8 PM' rule became their unexpected game-changer. Within weeks, they noticed increased emotional attunement and fewer misunderstandings.

Unity is the bedrock of a thriving Christian marriage. Through embracing individuality, practicing selfless love, effective communication, conflict resolution, prayer, and daily acts of unity, couples can build a harmonious and God-honouring partnership. As husbands and wives actively cultivate unity, they leave a legacy of love and faithfulness for their children and future generations to follow.

Remember, with God at the centre, unity becomes an enduring reality, making a Christian marriage a powerful witness to the world of God's transformative love.

---

48 Wilcox, W. B., & Dew, J. (2023). The Date Night Opportunity: What Does Couple Time Tell Us About the Potential Value of Date Nights? National Marriage Project. Retrieved from https://nationalmarriageproject.org/sites/g/files/jsddwu1276/files/inline-files/NMP-DateNightReport_2023-Final-Copy.pdf

UNITY IS THE BEDROCK OF A THRIVING CHRISTIAN MARRIAGE

REFLECTION QUESTIONS FOR COUPLES

1. In what areas do you and your spouse think differently? How can you bridge that gap?

2. What habits do you need to change to promote unity?

3. How do you handle disagreements—do you fight to win, or to understand?

CASE STUDY:
PETER AND JANE – CLASH OF CULTURES

Peter was a planner. Raised in a military home, everything from breakfast to bedtime followed a schedule. Jane was the opposite. She danced through life with spontaneous joy, often making plans at the last minute and changing them twice. Their personalities, while attractive at first, soon became battlegrounds.

Their arguments were frequent, especially over finances and parenting styles. Peter felt Jane was irresponsible; Jane felt Peter was controlling. One night, after a fight about vacation plans, Jane said, 'I feel like I have to stop being me to stay married to you.' The room went quiet.

That sentence hung heavy in Peter's heart. Was he asking Jane to lose herself? The following day, he picked up his Bible and read 1 Corinthians 12:14: 'The body is not made up of one part but many.' The scripture pierced his pride. God didn't create uniformity in unity – He created diversity.

Peter sat Jane down that evening and apologised. They began the hard work of understanding each other's wiring. Instead of resisting their differences, they looked for ways to combine them. Jane brought joy and flexibility to their home; Peter brought order and structure. Together, they were stronger.

They began a 'unity ritual': 10 minutes each night of intentional, uninterrupted connection – sharing wins, worries, and words of appreciation. Over time, the tension melted. Arguments became discussions. They started praying together and dreaming again.

Unity, they discovered, wasn't about becoming the same. It was about walking in the same direction—together.

ENCOURAGEMENT

Your differences are not your enemy. They are God's design to teach you grace, patience, and power in partnership. Unity is forged when two unique people choose to move as one.

4

———

Intimacy

4

INTIMACY

Our souls crave intimacy.

ERWIN RAPHAEL MCMANUS [49]

True intimacy in marriage is a profound and multifaceted connection that goes far beyond physical closeness. It is the deep, soul-level bond that unites a husband and wife emotionally, intellectually, spiritually, and physically.

Intimacy in marriage is all about building a deep, meaningful connection with your partner. It's not just about physical intimacy, although that's certainly an important aspect of it. It's also about emotional intimacy, intellectual intimacy, and spiritual intimacy.

---

49 McManus, E. R. How important is intimacy in a relationship. Marriage.com. Retrieved from https://www.marriage.com/advice/intimacy/how-important -is-intimacy-in-a-relationship/

The Bible provides a foundational understanding of intimacy in marriage. The Bible says:

> *"The husband should fulfill his marital*
> *duty to his wife, and likewise the wife*
> *to her husband. The wife does not have*
> *authority over her own body but yields*
> *it to her husband. In the same way,*
> *the husband does not have authority*
> *over his own body but yields it to his wife."*
>
> I CORINTHIANS 7:3-5 (NIV) [50]

This emphasises mutual self-giving, where both spouses are called to nurture and cherish one another in every dimension of their relationship. Of course, modern research supports this biblical principle, revealing that couples who cultivate all aspects of intimacy experience greater marital satisfaction, stronger conflict resolution skills, and a deeper sense of lifelong fulfilment.

According to a report by the Wheatley Institute, couples who devote time specifically to dating one another at least once or twice a month are markedly more likely to report better relationship quality compared to couples who do not go on dates as often [51].

---

50 1 Corinthians 7:3-5 (NIV) – The Holy Bible

51 PR Newswire. (2023, February 14). *Date nights linked to stronger marriages, more sexual satisfaction, according to new study.* PR Newswire. Retrieved from https://www.prnewswire.com/news-releases/date-nights-linked-to-stronger -marriages-more-sexual-satisfaction-according-to-new-study-301742711

THE ILLUSION OF INTIMACY: RECONSIDERING THE LINK BETWEEN SEX AND LOVE

In our modern world, the concept of intimacy has been erroneously linked solely to sexual encounters. However, true intimacy involves much more than physical attraction. While sex is a beautiful expression of love within marriage, it cannot stand alone as a definitive proof of love.

Intimacy is rooted in emotional and spiritual connections that form the foundation of a lasting and meaningful relationship. We all crave intimacy, and physical contact can provide the illusion of intimacy for a brief period of time. But that is not all to intimacy in marriage.

When it comes to true intimacy, it's not just about having sex. Jesus said;

"And these two shall become one..."
MARK 10:8 [52]

I'm convinced that Jesus had something more in mind than just the physical when He said that. Then again, there are many couples who share their bodies but not their hearts when they go to bed at night. Loneliness is a common complaint among this kind of people as they feel disconnected from their partner.

You see, sex is only an outlet (or vehicle) for intimacy because it is not its source. As long as there is no emotional

---

52 Mark 10:8 (NKJV), The Holy Bible – "And the two shall become one flesh; so then they are no longer two, but one flesh."

FOUR PILLARS: ESSENTIAL ELEMENTS FOR MARRIAGE

or spiritual intimacy before sex, there will be no intimacy afterwards.

WHEN IT COMES TO TRUE INTIMACY, IT'S NOT JUST ABOUT HAVING SEX

Source of Intimacy in Marriage

Intimacy in marriage finds its ultimate source in two interconnected aspects: a relationship with God and a special person who shares life's journey. Both elements are foundational to building a deep and meaningful connection in Marriage.

A solid relationship with God lays the groundwork for intimacy in marriage. As individuals draw closer to God, they experience His unconditional love, grace, and guidance. This, in turn, shapes their ability to love and connect with their spouse on a deeper level.

Here's how a relationship with God fuels intimacy:

• Understanding Unconditional Love

God's love is boundless and unconditional. As individuals experience God's love, they learn to extend that same love to their spouse, regardless of imperfections or shortcomings. This unconditional love fosters emotional intimacy and a safe space for vulnerability.

• Strengthening Emotional and Spiritual Connection

As couples grow together in their faith, they develop a shared spiritual connection. This shared spiritual journey strengthens the emotional bond between them as they support and encourage each other's growth in God.

• Seeking God's Guidance in Marriage

Inviting God into the marriage brings wisdom and direction. When couples seek God's guidance in their relationship, they cultivate a deeper understanding of each other's needs and desires, leading to a more fulfilling and harmonious union.

> *"And so we know and rely on the love*
> *God has for us. God is love. Whoever lives*
> *in love lives in God, and God in them."*
> I JOHN 4:16 [53]

Subsequently, there is an inseparable connection between God and love. When individuals dwell in God's love, that love permeates their relationships, including their marriage.

Furthermore, the second source of intimacy in marriage is the presence of a special person who walks beside you in life's journey. This person becomes a confidant, a friend, and a partner who lightens the burdens of life.

This special person in marriage provides companionship and emotional support through life's ups and downs. Sharing

---

53 1 John 4:16 (NKJV), The Holy Bible – "And we have known and believed the love that God has for us. God is love, and he who abides in love abides in God, and God in him."

joys, sorrows, and everything in between builds a deep emotional connection.

Of course, couples in marriage ought to be there for each other to uplift and affirm one another. This encouragement nurtures emotional intimacy and strengthens the bond of trust between partners. A special person in marriage brings joy and humour into the relationship, allowing both partners to experience genuine delight and closeness.

"A friend loves at all times, and a brother
is born in a time of adversity."
PROVERBS 17:17 [54]

Your special person in marriage embodies the role of a friend, providing love and support through all seasons of life.

When God is at the centre of the relationship, and two hearts are intertwined in love and support, intimacy flourishes, and the marriage becomes a testimony to the beauty of God's design for union and love.

WHEN INDIVIDUALS DWELL IN GOD'S LOVE, THAT LOVE PERMEATES THEIR RELATIONSHIPS, INCLUDING THEIR MARRIAGE

---

54 Proverbs 17:17 (NKJV), The Holy Bible – "A friend loves at all times, and a brother is born for adversity."

The Four Dimensions of Marital Intimacy

Marital intimacy can be broken down into four essential dimensions, each playing a critical role in sustaining a thriving marriage.

• Spiritual Intimacy

This type of intimacy involves sharing one's spiritual beliefs and values with their partner. It can include praying together, attending church or religious services, and engaging in discussions about faith and spirituality. Spiritual intimacy is about deepening the connection between partners on a spiritual level and growing together in their faith.

Cultivating spiritual intimacy is vital in Christian marriages. It involves sharing one's faith, beliefs, and values with their partner. Engaging in spiritual activities together, such as praying, attending church or religious services, and discussing matters of faith, deepens the connection between partners on a spiritual level.

When both spouses are aligned in their spiritual journey, they can support and encourage each other in their faith walk. Sharing a common purpose in Christ strengthens the marital bond, enabling couples to weather life's challenges hand-in-hand.

> *"Two are better than one because they have a good return for their labor. For if either of them falls, the one will lift up his companion. But woe to the one who falls when there is not another to lift him up. Furthermore, if two lie down together,*

they keep warm, but how can one be warm alone?
And if one can overpower him who is alone,
two can resist him. A cord of three strands
is not quickly torn apart."
ECCLESIASTES 4:9-12 [55]

This beautiful passage emphasises the strength of unity in marriage. The cord of three strands symbolizes the intertwining of God, husband, and wife in a covenant relationship. When spiritual intimacy is nurtured, this trifold bond becomes unbreakable, enabling couples to support and uplift each other through life's trials.

The foundation of spiritual intimacy lies in sharing a common faith and beliefs. When both spouses have a shared understanding of their faith, they can walk together in alignment with God's principles for marriage.

"Do two walk together unless
they have agreed to do so?"
AMOS 3:3 [56]

When couples are in agreement and walk together in harmony, they can cultivate spiritual intimacy and grow closer to God and each other.

More so, prayer is a powerful tool that fosters spiritual intimacy. Couples can pray together, seeking God's guidance and wisdom for their marriage and life journey. Engaging in

---

55 Ecclesiastes 4:9-12 (NKJV), The Holy Bible

56 Amos 3:3 (NKJV), The Holy Bible – "Can two walk together, unless they are agreed?"

worship together also strengthens their spiritual connection, drawing them closer to God as they exalt Him in unity.

"Again, truly I tell you that if two of you
on earth agree about anything they ask for,
it will be done for them by my Father
in heaven. For where two or three gather
in my name, there am I with them."
MATTHEW 18:19-20 [57]

When a husband and wife come together in prayer, they tap into the promise of Christ's presence among them. Their unity in prayer invites God's divine guidance and blessings into their marriage.

Supporting each other's spiritual growth is an essential aspect of spiritual intimacy. As each partner seeks to grow in their relationship with God, they can encourage and inspire one another to pursue a deeper connection with Him.

THE FOUNDATION OF SPIRITUAL INTIMACY LIES IN SHARING A COMMON FAITH AND BELIEFS

---

57 Matthew 18:19-20 (NKJV), The Holy Bible – "Again I say to you that if two of you agree on earth concerning anything that they ask, it will be done for them by My Father in heaven. For where two or three are gathered together in My name, I am there in the midst of them."

Mental or Emotional Intimacy

This type of intimacy involves sharing one's thoughts, feelings, and emotions with their partner. It can include having meaningful conversations, expressing vulnerability, and being open and honest with one another.

Mental or emotional intimacy is about connecting with your partner on an intellectual and emotional level and building a deep sense of trust and understanding. The Bible says:

"As iron sharpens iron,
so one person sharpens another."
PROVERBS 27:17 [58]

By being open and honest with one another, couples can build a deep sense of trust and understanding and grow together in their relationship.

THIS TYPE OF INTIMACY INVOLVES SHARING ONE'S THOUGHTS, FEELINGS, AND EMOTIONS WITH THEIR PARTNER

Cultivating Emotional Intimacy

Cultivating mental and emotional intimacy is a beautiful journey that deepens the bond between partners and strengthens the foundation of their marriage. It involves

---

58 Proverbs 27:17 (NKJV), The Holy Bible – "As iron sharpens iron, so a man sharpens the countenance of his friend."

sharing thoughts, feelings, and emotions in a safe and nurturing environment, allowing each other to be fully known and understood. Here are some practical steps to cultivate mental and emotional intimacy in your Marriage:

• **Create a Safe and Supportive Environment**

To foster mental and emotional intimacy, create an atmosphere of trust and support. Ensure that both partners feel safe expressing their thoughts and emotions without fear of judgment or criticism. Listen actively and attentively when your spouse speaks, validating their feelings and experiences.

• **Engage in Meaningful Conversations**

Take the time to have deep and meaningful conversations with your spouse. Ask open-ended questions that encourage reflection and sharing. Discuss your dreams, fears, and aspirations, and be genuinely interested in each other's perspectives.

• **Be Vulnerable and Share Your Feelings**

Vulnerability is essential in cultivating emotional intimacy. Be willing to share your true feelings and emotions with your partner. Expressing vulnerability fosters a deeper connection and allows your spouse to understand your needs and desires.

• **Practice Empathy and Understanding**

Show empathy and understanding towards your partner's feelings and experiences. Try to put yourself in their shoes and see things from their perspective. Empathy nurtures emotional intimacy and builds a stronger emotional connection.

• Be Present and Available

Be emotionally present and available for your spouse. Put away distractions and give them your undivided attention when they need to talk. Show your support through both words and actions.

• Resolve Conflicts with Respect

Conflicts are a natural part of any relationship, but it's essential to handle them with respect and compassion. Avoid blame and criticism, focus on finding solutions together. Working through conflicts constructively strengthens emotional intimacy.

• Share Laughter and Joy

Emotional intimacy also involves sharing moments of joy and laughter. Find opportunities to have fun together, engage in activities that make you both happy and create cherished memories.

• Grow Together Spiritually

Nurturing your spiritual life as a couple can also deepen emotional intimacy. Pray together, study the Scriptures, and attend spiritual events or retreats. Growing spiritually as a team strengthens your bond and shared purpose.

• Be Patient and Understanding

Building emotional intimacy takes time and effort. Be patient with each other as you navigate the ups and downs of life together. Understanding that intimacy grows over time allows you to nurture it with love and care.

• Show Appreciation and Affection

Express appreciation and affection for your spouse regularly. Simple gestures like compliments, hugs, and acts of kindness strengthen the emotional connection between you.

> *"Love is patient; love is kind. It does not envy; it does not boast, it is not proud. It does not dishonour others; it is not self-seeking, it is not easily angered, and it keeps no record of wrongs. Love does not delight in evil but rejoices with the truth. It always protects, always trusts, always hopes, always perseveres."*
>
> I CORINTHIANS 13:4-7 [59]

Love, the foundation of intimacy, requires patience, kindness, and the willingness to protect and trust each other.

WORKING THROUGH CONFLICTS CONSTRUCTIVELY STRENGTHENS EMOTIONAL INTIMACY

PHYSICAL INTIMACY

This type of intimacy involves the sexual and physical connection between partners. It can include intimacy, hugging, kissing, and sexual activity. Physical intimacy is about connecting with your partner on a physical level and building a deep sense of trust and closeness.

---

59 1 Corinthians 13:4-7 (NKJV), The Holy Bible

FOUR PILLARS: ESSENTIAL ELEMENTS FOR MARRIAGE

The Bible also acknowledges the importance of physical intimacy in marriage according to I Corinthians 7:3-5. It states that husbands and wives should not deprive one another of physical intimacy and that they should come together regularly. This implies that physical intimacy can help couples build a deep sense of closeness and strengthen their bond.

God designed physical intimacy as a sacred and beautiful expression of love and unity within marriage. It is an intimate union that mirrors the deep oneness between Christ and His Church.

> *"That is why a man leaves his father*
> *and mother and is united to his wife,*
> *and they become one flesh."*
> GENESIS 2:24 [60]

The first marriage between Adam and Eve establishes the divine blueprint for physical intimacy, which God intended for husband and wife to become one in every aspect of their being, including physical union.

"GOD DESIGNED PHYSICAL INTIMACY AS A SACRED AND BEAUTIFUL EXPRESSION OF LOVE AND UNITY WITHIN MARRIAGE"

---

60 Genesis 2:24 (NKJV), The Holy Bible

INTELLECTUAL INTIMACY

Intellectual intimacy—the shared life of the mind between husband and wife—is both a bonding agent and a catalyst for growth within marriage. Though it may not receive as much attention as emotional or physical intimacy, this thoughtful connection is equally essential for lasting satisfaction in the relationship.

Intellectual intimacy flourishes when couples:

+ **Cultivate shared curiosity** – Embracing life with a *'let's discover together'* mindset.

+ **Practice active perspective-taking** – Making the intentional effort to understand each other's thoughts, beliefs, and viewpoints.

+ **Create meaning through dialogue** – Engaging in conversations that go beyond surface-level exchange, becoming opportunities for learning, insight, and mutual enrichment.

This form of intimacy has little to do with academic credentials or intellectual status. Whether one holds a PhD or works a trade, intellectual intimacy isn't about how much you know—it's about *how you connect through what you think and how you grow together mentally*. It's the intentional engagement with one another's inner worlds that sets this apart and strengthens the foundation of the marriage.

In the garden of marriage, intellectual intimacy is the often-overlooked vine quietly weaving strength, stability, and depth into the union. While emotional and physical connection may steal the spotlight, it is the *life of the mind shared between spouses* that often determines whether a couple thrives or merely survives.

The importance of intellectual nourishment cannot be overstated. It's the daily brain-to-brain engagement that keeps the relationship vibrant, evolving, and rooted. And understanding *why* it matters makes all the difference.

1. Prevents Mental Drift

Just as muscles weaken without regular use, so too can a relationship lose its tone without mental exercise. When couples stop learning together, they risk drifting apart intellectually, becoming strangers in the same home. But when they stimulate each other's minds—through curiosity, exploration, and meaningful dialogue—they remain mentally engaged and emotionally tethered.

2. Builds Cognitive Empathy

Something powerful happens when partners consistently share thoughts, ideas, and insights: they start to develop what neuroscientists call 'shared neural pathways.' In simple terms, their brains begin to align. They anticipate each other's responses, finish each other's sentences, and intuitively understand one another's reasoning. This mental harmony fosters deeper emotional connection and makes communication richer and more efficient.

3. Creates Future Alignment

Couples who think together tend to *move* together. When intellectual intimacy is cultivated, spouses are better equipped to:

+ Make wise financial decisions with shared reasoning and trust

+ Parent with consistency, drawing from a united mental framework

+ Navigate life's changes—career shifts, aging parents, retirement—without falling out of sync

This alignment doesn't happen by accident. It's the fruit of deliberate, ongoing engagement with each other's ideas, values, dreams, and concerns.

In my experience, **intellectual intimacy is the unsung hero of enduring marriages.** It's the quiet difference between couples who coexist out of habit and those who continue to *discover* one another with joy and wonder. It fuels a kind of friendship that goes far beyond routine—one where each new conversation holds the possibility of surprise, laughter, and growth.

And here's the beautiful truth: **it's never too late to begin.** Whether you've been married for two years or forty, the next honest, curious, open-hearted conversation could mark the beginning of a whole new chapter in your relationship—one defined by shared learning, mutual respect, and a renewed connection of the mind and soul.

INTELLECTUAL INTIMACY – THE SHARED LIFE OF THE MIND BETWEEN PARTNERS – SERVES AS BOTH GLUE AND GROWTH ACCELERATOR IN MARRIAGE

Case Study:
David and Ruth – Restoring Lost Intimacy

David and Ruth (names changed for privacy) had been married for ten years when they realised their relationship was in trouble. With three young children, demanding careers, and mounting financial pressures, they had slowly stopped prioritising each other.

Their conversations became transactional – focused solely on parenting duties and household logistics – while their emotional and physical connection dwindled. Ruth later admitted, 'We were living under the same roof, but we felt completely alone.' Their breaking point came after a heated argument where both confessed to feeling unloved and disconnected. Recognising the severity of their situation, they sought help from a Christian marriage counsellor, who guided them in rebuilding their intimacy step by step.

The counsellor helped them understand that true intimacy is not automatic – it requires intentional effort. David and Ruth committed to a structured plan that included weekly

date nights without distractions, daily prayer together, and intentional conversations that went beyond surface-level discussions.

Within six months, they began to see a dramatic shift. 'Praying together softened our hearts toward each other,' David shared. 'And setting aside time to really talk reminded me why I fell in love with her in the first place.'

David and Ruth's story shows that intimacy isn't lost – it's simply waiting to be rediscovered. Like many couples, they had allowed life's demands to erode their connection, but through humility, commitment, and guided effort, they rebuilt what was broken. Whether through prayer, purposeful conversation, or protected time together, the solution to emotional drift lies in intentional acts of love. For any couple feeling distant, take heart: what David and Ruth restored is possible for you, too.

As Ecclesiastes 4:12 promises, 'A cord of three strands is not quickly broken.' When God is at the centre, even the most frayed bonds can be rewoven into something stronger than before.

Fostering Intimacy in All Seasons of Marriage

Intimacy is sweet at the beginning, but gives couples reasons to rethink when childbearing starts. The presence of children in any home brings immense joy and fulfilment to a marriage, but it also introduces new challenges to maintaining intimacy between partners.

As parents, it's essential to find ways to balance the responsibilities of parenting while nurturing the emotional and physical connection with your spouse.

Here are some practical tips for fostering intimacy in the midst of parenting:

• Prioritise Quality Time Together

In the midst of busy parenting schedules, make it a priority to set aside quality time for each other. Whether it's a date night out or a cozy evening at home after the kids are asleep, spending focused time together strengthens your emotional bond.

• Communicate Openly About Your Needs

Be open and honest with your spouse about your emotional and physical needs. Effective communication is the key to understanding each other's feelings and desires. Expressing your needs allows both of you to work together in finding solutions to maintain intimacy.

• Support Each Other's Parenting Roles

Acknowledge and appreciate each other's efforts as parents. Support each other in your respective parenting roles, and work as a team in making decisions for your children. A united front in parenting strengthens the marital bond.

• Schedule Regular Date Nights

Set aside designated date nights on a regular basis, even if it means arranging for childcare. Date nights provide an opportunity to reconnect as a couple and enjoy each other's company without the distractions of parenting responsibilities.

• Express Affection and Appreciation
Show affection and appreciation for each other regularly. Simple gestures like hugging, holding hands, or complimenting each other go a long way in nurturing intimacy.

• Be Flexible and Understanding
Parenting can be unpredictable, and plans may change at the last minute. Be flexible and understanding when unexpected situations arise. Embrace the ebb and flow of parenthood together.

• Create Moments of Intimacy
Find opportunities to create moments of intimacy amidst your parenting routine. It could be a shared morning coffee before the kids wake up, a heartfelt conversation after the children are in bed, or a spontaneous hug during a busy day.

• Preserve Your Physical Connection
Even with the demands of parenting, make an effort to preserve your physical connection. Hold hands, cuddle on the couch, or share affectionate gestures to reinforce your emotional bond.

• Communicate About Your Feelings
Be open about how parenting has impacted your emotional connection. Sharing your feelings with your spouse fosters understanding and allows both of you to work together in strengthening intimacy.

In the pursuit of a lasting and fulfilling marriage, we must recognise that intimacy goes far beyond physical encounters. True intimacy is a multifaceted connection that encompasses emotional, intellectual, and spiritual aspects. It is a union of hearts and souls that stands the test of time, anchored in the love of God and the profound bond between two individuals.

As we embrace intimacy in its fullest sense, we discover that it is not a destination but an ever-evolving adventure – an adventure of love, trust, and shared dreams. A beautiful tapestry woven by the Creator Himself. In the depths of this intimacy, we find the true essence of marriage – a divine union that mirrors the love between Christ and His Church. A love that endures and stands the test of time, shining brightly for all to see.

So, let us embark on this journey of intimacy, knowing that it will be challenging at times, but it is in the journey that we truly discover the beauty and depth of the love that binds us together as one

FIND OPPORTUNITIES TO CREATE MOMENTS OF INTIMACY AMIDST YOUR PARENTING ROUTINE

REFLECTION QUESTIONS FOR COUPLES

1. Which area of intimacy (spiritual, emotional, physical) needs the most attention in your marriage?

2. How do work, children, or social media affect intimacy in your relationship?

3. What is one practical step you will take this week to reconnect with your spouse?

CASE STUDY:
CHINEDU AND ADA – TOGETHER BUT APART

From the outside, Chinedu and Ada were the picture-perfect couple. He was a respected engineer; she was a beloved teacher. They attended church faithfully and hosted guests with smiles. But behind closed doors, they felt like roommates.

Their conversations were limited to logistics – kids, bills, work schedules. Their sex life had become mechanical. Ada often lay in bed wondering, 'Is this all marriage is?' She longed to be pursued, seen, desired, not just physically, but emotionally. Chinedu, though not unloving, was exhausted. Providing for the family drained him. He didn't realise how distant he'd become.

One evening, Ada broke down in tears after another silent dinner. 'I miss us,' she whispered. 'I don't want sex – I want connection.' That sentence undid Chinedu. For the first time, he realised that intimacy was not just about physical closeness but about knowing and being known.

They took a bold step. They unplugged their evenings – no phones, no distractions. They started journaling together and sharing their entries weekly. They prayed together before bed. Chinedu surprised Ada with handwritten notes, and Ada began affirming Chinedu's efforts without criticism.

After laughing over old memories one night, Chinedu reached for Ada, not out of duty but desire. This time, their intimacy wasn't forced. It was a byproduct of emotional closeness, safety, and trust.

Today, their intimacy is more profound than ever. Not because they found new techniques but because they rediscovered the beauty of oneness in spirit, soul, and body.

Encouragement

True intimacy starts before the bedroom. It begins with connection, kindness, shared vulnerability, and God at the centre. When hearts touch, bodies follow—and intimacy becomes sacred again.

CONCLUSION

Conclusion

In conclusion, the institution of marriage was created by God and can only be sustained by Him. The four essential elements of marriage discussed in this book are crucial to building a strong and lasting relationship with your spouse. When these elements are present and nurtured in a marriage, it can be a beautiful and fulfilling journey of growth and love. Remember that building a blissful home starts with allowing God into your relationship and following His design for marriage.

BUILDING WITH THE FOUR PILLARS

*"Therefore everyone who hears
these words of Mine and puts them
into practice is like a wise man who
built his house on the rock."*

MATTHEW 7:24 (NIV)[61]

marriage is more than a ceremony, a shared home, or a legal contract – it is a covenant. It is a divine partnership between a man and a woman, built on a foundation designed and sustained by God Himself.

In this book, we explored four essential pillars: **Severance, Permanence, Unity, and Intimacy.** Like the four legs of a table, each pillar must be firm and rightly placed for the marriage to stand strong and support the weight of life's seasons.

1. Severance – The First Step Toward Oneness

A man must leave – physically, emotionally, financially, and spiritually – to cleave. Severance is not an act of dishonour but a declaration of adulthood and obedience. It's not about isolation from parents but about prioritisation of your spouse. Severance sets the stage for trust, leadership, and the beginning of a new lineage under God.

---

61 Matthew 7:24 (NIV), The Holy Bible

REFLECTION

+ Have I truly 'left' my family of origin in the ways God desires?

+ Are there emotional or financial dependencies that interfere with my marriage?

2. Permanence – The Anchor of Covenant Love

Marriage is not a contract to be terminated but a covenant to be honoured. When God joins a couple, He intends for them to remain together. Permanence is not sustained by feelings but by faithfulness. It is a decision to stay, to love, and to forgive – even when it hurts.

REFLECTION

+ Is my view of marriage shaped more by culture or by Scripture?

+ How am I nurturing a sense of permanence in my relationship daily?

3. Unity – Becoming One in Heart and Purpose

Unity is the visible fruit of an invisible bond. It is more than agreement; it is alignment. Through humility, patience, and shared purpose, a husband and wife become one flesh, not only physically but spiritually and emotionally. Unity doesn't mean uniformity; it means harmony.

REFLECTION

+ Are we fighting for oneness or individual agendas?

+ In what areas can I better support our unity—spiritually, emotionally, or practically?

4. Intimacy – The Fruit of Deep Connection

True intimacy is not just physical; it is also emotional, intellectual, and spiritual. It is cultivated through shared prayer, meaningful communication, and sacrificial love. Intimacy flows from safety, trust, and time invested.

REFLECTION

+ Are we growing in more profound understanding and closeness?

+ Have we created a safe space for vulnerability, affection, and shared spirituality?

A Marriage that Mirrors Heaven

Each of these pillars reflects the nature of Christ and the Church:

+ *Severance mirrors Jesus leaving heaven to redeem us.*

+ *Permanence reflects His unwavering commitment.*

+ *Unity is seen in His Union with the Church.*

+ *Intimacy is found in the closeness He invites us into as His Bride.*

Your marriage is not just about you; it is a testimony to the world. When a marriage is built on these four pillars, it becomes a beacon of light in a world plagued by relational confusion and brokenness.

TAKE ACTION: BUILDING ON THE ROCK

"Unless the Lord builds the house,
those who build it labor in vain."
PSALM 127:1[62]

Don't just admire these pillars; use them to build a rock solid foundation for your marriage:

+ Pray together consistently and intentionally. Make Christ your cornerstone.

+ Set boundaries with external influences —whether family, work, or distractions— that threaten your severance and unity.

+ Reaffirm your vows, in word and in practice. Say 'I do' not just at the altar but in your actions each day.

+ Invest in your intimacy. Take time to be present, affectionate, and emotionally available.

+ Surround your marriage with the community. A godly village helps you stay accountable and encouraged.

---

62 Psalm 127:1 (NIV), The Holy Bible

A FINAL WORD OF HOPE

No marriage is perfect, but every marriage surrendered to God can be made new.

If one or more pillars in your marriage feel shaky, you don't need to tear down the whole house. Start rebuilding today… slowly, intentionally, and prayerfully. God is a restorer. His grace is sufficient. His Word is your blueprint.

You are not building alone. With God as your foundation, your marriage can become all He intended it to be – a beautiful, enduring reflection of His covenant love.

GOD IS A RESTORER

References

References

CHAPTER 1: SEVERANCE

BIBLICAL REFERENCES

- Genesis 2:24 (NKJV), The Holy Bible – "That is why a man leaves his father and mother and is joined to his wife, and they become one flesh."

- Genesis 1:26 (NKJV), The Holy Bible
  Then God said, "Let Us make man in Our image, according to Our likeness; let them have dominion over the fish of the sea, over the birds of the air, and over the cattle, over all the earth and over every creeping thing that creeps on the earth."

- Matthew 19:6 (NKJV), The Holy Bible – "So then, they are no longer two but one flesh. Therefore what God has joined together, let not man separate."

- 1 Samuel 25: 44 (NKJV), The Holy Bible – "But Saul had given Michal, his daughter, David's wife, to Palti, the son of Laish, who was from Gallim."

- Exodus 20:12 (NKJV), The Holy Bible – "Honour your father and your mother, that your days may be long upon the land which the Lord your God is giving you."

- Mark 10:8 (NKJV), The Holy Bible – "…And the two shall become one flesh, so then they are no longer two, but one flesh."

STATISTICAL REFERENCES

- American Association for Marriage and Family Therapy. (n.d.). About marriage and family therapists. AAMFT. Retrieved March 27, 2025, from https://www.aamft.org/AAMFT/About_AAMFT/About_Marriage_and_Family_Therapists.aspx

- Pew Research Center. (2024, January 25). Financial help and independence in young adulthood. Pew Research Center. Retrieved from https://www.pewresearch.org/social-trends/2024/01/25/financial-help-and-independence-in-young-adulthood/

◆ Mammen, K. (2020). Children's gender and investments from nonresident fathers. Journal of Family and Economic Issues, 41, 332-349.

◆ Monk, J. K., Bordere, T. C., & Benson, J. J. (2021). Emerging ideas. Advancing family science through public scholarship: Fostering community relationships and engaging in broader impacts. Family Relations, 70(5), 1612-1625.

◆ Sheidlower, N. (2024, January 27). Most parents are still giving money to their young adult kids, survey found. Business Insider Africa. Retrieved March 27, 2025, from https://africa.businessinsider.com/news/most-parents-are-still-giving-money-to-their-young-adult-kids-survey-found/b1grwmr

CHAPTER 2: PERMANENCE

BIBLICAL REFERENCES

◆ Mark 10:9 (NKJV), The Holy Bible – "Therefore what God has joined together, let not man separate."

◆ Genesis 2:24 (NKJV), The Holy Bible.

◆ Matthew 19:9 (NKJV), The Bible – "Whoever divorces his wife, except for sexual immorality, and marries another, commits adultery; and whoever marries her who is divorced commits adultery

◆ Psalm 15:4 (NKJV), The Holy Bible – "Who keeps an oath even when it hurts, and does not change their mind."

+ Ephesians 4:2-3 (NKJV) – The Bible

+ Hosea 1:2 (NKJV) – The Bible

+ Hosea 3:1-2 (NKJV) – The Bible

+ Malachi 3:6 (NKJV), The Holy Bible – "For I am the Lord, I do not change; Therefore you are not consumed, O sons of Jacob."

+ 1 Corinthians 7:10-11 (NKJV), The Holy Bible – "A wife is not to depart from her husband... And a husband is not to divorce his wife."

+ Malachi 2:16 (NLT) – The Holy Bible

STATISTICAL REFERENCES

+ American Psychological Association. (2013, April). Can this marriage be saved? Monitor on Psychology, 44(4). Retrieved from https://www.apa.org/monitor/2013/04/marriage

+ Forbes Advisor. Revealing Divorce Statistics In 2025. Forbes. Retrieved March 27, 2025, from https://www.forbes.com/advisor/legal/divorce/divorce-statistics/

CHAPTER 3: UNITY

BIBLICAL REFERENCES

+ 1 Corinthians 12:14 (NKJV), The Holy Bible – "For in fact, the body is not one member but many."

+ Ruth 1:16 (NKJV), The Holy Bible – "Where you go, I will go, and where you stay, I will stay. Your people will be my people, and your God my God."

+ 1 Corinthians 12:12 (NKJV), The Holy Bible – "For as the body is one and has many members, but all the members of that one body, being many, are one body, so also is Christ."

+ Mark 10:8 (NKJV), The Holy Bible.

+ Proverbs 9:10 (NKJV), The Holy Bible – "The fear of the Lord is the beginning of wisdom, and the knowledge of the Holy One is understanding."

+ 1 Corinthians 7:33-34 (NKJV), The Holy Bible – "But he who is married cares about the things of the world—how he may please his wife."

+ Genesis 2:23 (NKJV), The Holy Bible – "This is now bone of my bones and flesh of my flesh; she shall be called 'woman,' for she was taken out of man."

+ Ecclesiastes 4:9-11 (NKJV), The Holy Bible

+ 1 Peter 4:10 (NKJV), The Holy Bible – "As each has received a gift, use it to serve one another, as good stewards of God's varied grace."

+ Philippians 2:3-4 (NIV), The Holy Bible – "Do nothing out of selfish ambition or vain conceit. Rather, in humility value others above yourselves, not looking to your own interests but each of you to the interests of the others."

Statistical References

+ Gottman Institute. Marriage and Couples. The Gottman Institute. Retrieved March 27, 2025, from https://www.gottman.com/about/research/couples/

+ Dodds, R. C. The goal in marriage is not to think alike, but to think together. Marriage.com. Retrieved from https://www.marriage.com/quotes/4

+ Stanton, G. (2018). Does faith reduce divorce risk? The Public Discourse. Retrieved from https://www.thepublicdiscourse.com/2018/03/20935/

+ Human Flourishing Programme at Harvard University. (2018). Religious service attendance, divorce, and remarriage among U.S. nurses in mid – and late-life. Retrieved from https://hfh.fas.harvard.edu/news/human-flourishing-program-releases-new-study-divorce

+ Wilcox, W. B., & Dew, J. (2023). The Date Night Opportunity: What Does Couple Time Tell Us About the Potential Value of Date Nights? National Marriage Project. Retrieved from https://nationalmarriageproject.org/sites/g/files/jsddwu1276/files/inline-files/NMP-DateNightReport_2023-Final-Copy.pdf

CHAPTER 4: INTIMACY

BIBLICAL REFERENCES

- 1 Corinthians 7:3-5 (NIV), The Holy Bible

- Mark 10:8 (NKJV), The Holy Bible – "And the two shall become one flesh; so then they are no longer two, but one flesh."

- 1 John 4:16 (NKJV), The Holy Bible – "And we have known and believed the love that God has for us. God is love, and he who abides in love abides in God, and God in him."

- Proverbs 17:17 (NKJV), The Holy Bible – "A friend loves at all times, and a brother is born for adversity."

- Ecclesiastes 4:9-12 (NKJV), The Holy Bible – "Two are better than one, because they have a good reward for their labor. For if they fall, one will lift up his companion. But woe to him who is alone when he falls, for he has no one to help him up. Again, if two lie down together, they will keep warm; but how can one be warm alone? Though one may be overpowered by another, two can withstand him. And a threefold cord is not quickly broken."

- Amos 3:3 (NKJV), The Holy Bible – "Can two walk together, unless they are agreed?"

- Matthew 18:19-20 (NKJV), The Holy Bible – "Again I say to you that if two of you agree on earth concerning anything that they ask, it will be done for them by My Father in heaven. For where two or three are gathered together in My name, I am there in the midst of them."

+ Proverbs 27:17 (NKJV), The Holy Bible – "As iron sharpens iron, so a man sharpens the countenance of his friend."

STATISTICAL REFERENCES

+ McManus, E. R. How important is intimacy in a relationship. Marriage.com. Retrieved from https://www.marriage.com/advice/intimacy/how-important-is-intimacy-in-a-relationship/

+ PR Newswire. (2023, February 14). Date nights linked to stronger marriages, more sexual satisfaction, according to new study. PR Newswire. Retrieved from https://www.prnewswire.com/news-releases/date-nights-linked-to-stronger-marriages-more-sexual-satisfaction-according-to-new-study-301742711

OTHER BOOKS
BY THE AUTHOR

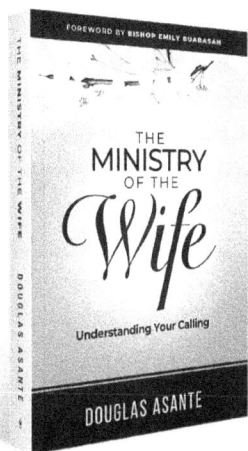

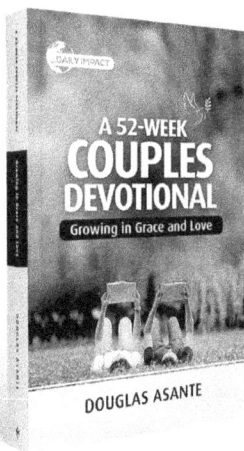

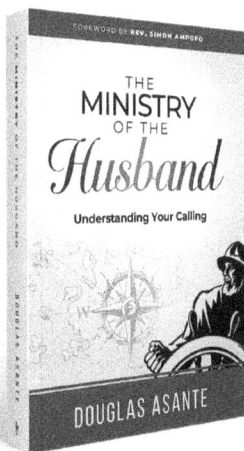

FOREWORD BY BISHOP EMILY OUABASAH

THE
MINISTRY
OF THE
Wife

Understanding Your Calling

DOUGLAS ASANTE

DAILY IMPACT

A 52-WEEK
COUPLES
DEVOTIONAL
Growing in Grace and Love

DOUGLAS ASANTE

DAILY IMPACT

365
DAILY
DEVOTIONAL
Finding Inspiration and Purpose

DOUGLAS ASANTE

FOREWORD BY REV. SIMON AMPOFO

THE
MINISTRY
OF THE
Husband

Understanding Your Calling

DOUGLAS ASANTE

AVAILABLE ON
amazon   **amazon** kindle

www.dasante.org.uk

www.ingramcontent.com/pod-product-compliance
Lightning Source LLC
Chambersburg PA
CBHW030940090426
42737CB00007B/491